INTERNATIONAL SOCIALISM ★
A quarterly journal of socialist theory

Summer 2002
Contents

Issue 95 of INTERNATIONAL SOCIALISM, quarterly journal of the Socialist Workers Party (Britain)

Published July 2002
Copyright © International Socialism
Distribution/subscriptions: International Socialism,
PO Box 82, London E3 3LH
E-mail: isj@swp.org.uk
American distribution: B de Boer, 113 East Center Street, Nutley,
New Jersey 07110
US subscriptions: www.leftturnbooks.com
Editorial and production: 020 7538 5821
Sales and subscriptions: 020 7531 9810

ISBN 1 898876 88 6

Printed by BPC Wheatons Ltd, Exeter, England
Typeset by East End Offset, London E3
Cover design by Sherborne Design
Cover photograph by Jess Hurd (www.reportdigital.co.uk)

A full index for *International Socialism* is available at
www.lpi.org.uk
For details of back copies see the end pages of this book

Subscription rates for one year (four issues) are:

Britain and overseas (surface):	individual	£14 ($30)
	institutional	£25
Air speeded supplement:	North America	£2
	Europe/South America	£2
	elsewhere	£4

Note to contributors

The deadline for articles intended for issue 97 of *International Socialism* is 1 September 2002.

All contributions should be double spaced with wide margins. Please submit two copies. If you write your contribution using a computer, please also supply a disk, together with details of the computer and program used.

INTERNATIONAL SOCIALISM ★

A quarterly journal of socialist theory

RACE is once again at the centre of politics in Britain. New Labour's attacks on asylum seekers and the racist backlash against Muslims since 11 September have fuelled the far right, creating an atmosphere in which the Nazi BNP could gain three council seats in the north west mill town of Burnley. Hassan Mahamdallie lays bare the facts about racism in Britain, looking at the economic and social position of blacks and Asians in Britain today. With the first ever black cabinet minister in place, can New Labour offer a bulwark against racism? If not, what strategy should the left adopt?

LE PEN'S shock first round vote in the French presidential election was instantly met by spontaneous mass anti-fascist demonstrations on the streets of France. Jim Wolfreys looks at the history of Le Pen and the *Front National*, and argues that it was the collapse of the social democrat Jospin's vote, rather than a shift to the right in French politics, that was the crucial element in the election. He looks at the French left—now engaged in the most crucial debate for years—and argues for left unity.

LENIN'S THEORY of the revolutionary party has long been one of the most debated questions on the left. Here we print three articles on Leninism based on speeches given at the Marxism 2001 conference. Slavoj Žižek, author of *Did Somebody Say Totalitarianism?*, Daniel Bensaïd, a leading member of the Revolutionary Communist League in France, and John Rees, author of *The Algebra of Revolution*, put forward their views on the kind of organisation we need in the movement today.

PALESTINE has sparked a wave of demonstrations across the Middle East, throwing up the question of political leadership. Anne Alexander asks can the ideas of Arab nationalism or Islamism provide an answer, or is there now space for a new leadership to emerge?

BOOK REVIEWS include Tariq Ali's *The Clash of Fundamentalisms* and Paul Ginsborg's new history of contemporary Italy.

Editor: John Rees. Assistant editors: Alex Callinicos, Chris Harman, John Molyneux, Lindsey German, Colin Sparks, Mike Gonzalez, Peter Morgan, Jim Wolfreys, Mike Haynes, Judy Cox, Sally Campbell, Megan Trudell, Mark O'Brien, Michael Lavalette, Sam Ashman and Rob Hoveman.

Racism: myths and realities

HASSAN MAHAMDALLIE

Race is once again at the centre of politics in Britain. Half a century ago, during black immigration from the Commonwealth, there were early hopes in reformist quarters that strict immigration controls, combined with 'race' legislation to curb the worst aspects of prejudice, would result in racism fading away. The idea was that new arrivals would be gradually and benignly assimilated into the 'host' society. Such ideas have been shown to be wide of the mark. Although in general immigrants have sought to embrace the society they have found themselves in, they have been handicapped by racism that has blocked their path and that of their British-born children.

In the period following the publication of the Macpherson report after the racist murder of Stephen Lawrence there was a widespread sense of a new start—a watershed had been reached. Yet during the 2001 general election one of the Tories' strongest themes was racism towards asylum seekers. In government New Labour has played a double game of rhetoric about 'toleration' and 'inclusion' while enacting the harshest barrage of racist anti-asylum and anti-immigration measures seen for a generation.

The riots in the northern towns of Oldham, Burnley and Bradford in the summer of 2001, combined with the rise in racism towards Asians, especially Muslims, as a result of the 'war on terrorism' have produced a further step-change. We are seeing a racist 'blowback' from globalisation and imperialism. The intense racism against Muslims was typically articulated by *Daily Telegraph* editor Charles Moore. He declared that

'Britain is basically English speaking, Christian and white, and if one starts to think it might become basically Urdu speaking and Muslim and brown one gets frightened'.[1] The equivalent of Samuel Huntingdon's 'clash of civilisations'—that the West is superior to the East and that Islam is an expression of fundamentalist medievalism—has given an ideological shape to racist antagonisms on the ground in Oldham, Burnley, Bradford and elsewhere. This racism has been so pervasive that Asians, from wherever they come, or whatever religion they espouse, are now popularly portrayed as Muslims—as though the religion carried a racial type.

This racism towards Muslims comes on top of the intensification of 'Fortress Europe' anti-immigrant and anti asylum seeker racism. This has its roots in neo-liberal policies that are forcing increased displacement and migration of the world's poor due to the economic and military destruction of Third World and former Eastern Bloc countries. Governments across Europe have demonised a new scapegoat—asylum seekers and economic migrants, who have been cast as subhuman 'sewage'—'swamping' Europe. 'Swamping' was the term favoured by New Labour home secretary David Blunkett this year in an echo of Thatcher's notorious 1978 speech. This has led to brutal policies including the segregation of asylum seekers in camps, and mass deportations. These attacks have been combined with racist propaganda that asylum seekers are an external virus seeking to infect the otherwise healthy national body. This process of legitimising racism has fuelled a rise in fascist organisations—in Britain principally the British National Party (BNP). The same formula has been repeated across Western Europe, as the failure of centre-left reformist governments to deliver has seen them resort to the race card, only then to see themselves 'trumped' by the far right, dragging the debate further rightwards. The crisis of reformism has its reflection in every sphere of politics—race included.

These two planks of racism—against immigrants and Muslims—have been fused on an institutional level in Britain. New Labour home secretary David Blunkett has explicitly linked race with immigration, producing a new Nationality, Immigration and Asylum Bill in the wake of the riots. It combined an exclusive notion of British citizenship targeted at South Asians with a new battery of controls to stop blacks and the poor entering this country. Blunkett earned the plaudits of the BNP when, announcing new rules on citizenship in December 2001, he stated, 'We have norms of acceptability, and those who come into our home— for that is what it is—should accept those norms.' There are now new racist immigration controls that not only target migrants outside Britain's border, but simultaneously recast Asians who have lived in this country for decades (and their British-born offspring) as foreigners, who will only be tolerated if they forcibly assimilate 'British norms' and become in Blunkett's words 'more English'.

These victims of racism have been turned into the authors of their own oppression. New Labour's Europe minister Peter Hain blamed 'very isolationist' Muslims for the fact that black and Asian people face racial attacks. He joined the chorus of those who accuse Asians of 'self segregation' in the northern towns of England. Decades of racism, poverty and enforced division by the authorities have been conveniently whisked away. Instead problems in these areas are supposedly the result of the desires of Pakistanis and Bangladeshis to live in self-contained enclaves apart from 'white' society. The notion that a 'cultural divide' separates working class Asians from their white counterparts is now promoted both on the reformist left and the racist right. The report into the Oldham riots concluded that 'the main cause for residential segregation has been preferences both within the indigenous and Pakistani and Bangladeshi communities of people "to live with their own kind".'[2] Throughout history each new group of immigrants from 'races' deemed different (and inferior) to the majority has faced hostility and myths—the Irish in the 19th century, who were regarded as 'white niggers', the Jews who at the start of the 20th century were accused of refusing to integrate, and those coming from the Caribbean after the Second World War.

Myths of self segregation

There are many false arguments put forward about the root of the segregation of some Asian working class communities. For example, it is fallacious to generalise about the nature of the lives of people of Pakistani or Bangladeshi origin and their relations with their white counterparts solely from the experience of the mill towns. Most people from a Pakistani background live *outside* the north. Figures from the 1991 census showed that 29.9 percent of Pakistanis live in the south east of England, and 20.7 percent live in the West Midlands, compared with only 16.2 percent in the north west, and 19.9 percent in Yorkshire and Humberside.[3] The northern mill towns have seen a particular economic and social development resulting in enforced (not self) segregation from which it would be wrong to generalise. As Mohammed Anwar has argued, 'Their [Pakistanis'] position in the labour market is a fundamental aspect of their position in society. The type of work available to them on arrival not merely governed their incomes, it also determined in which areas they settled, where their children went to schools, their chances in participation in the civic life and their overall status in society'.[4]

In the 1960s Pakistani and later Bangladeshi male workers were encouraged to go to Lancashire and Yorkshire to work in the mills, doing the lowest paid and worst jobs (typically segregated night shift work). These immigrants were effectively barred from the council housing where white workers lived because of discrimination through residence qualifications and so settled in poor areas of dirt-cheap housing close to the textile mills. These included Oldham's Glodwick where Asians replaced Eastern European and black Caribbean workers who were in the process of moving out. Originally the predominantly male Asian workers held to the belief that they would return home after a few years. But this faded, and members of their close families—despite a succession of controls devised to keep them out—joined them over the next decade and a half. The gradual, but still far from total, isolation from white workers arose out of a number of factors connected not to their desire to live apart, but to their socio-economic position and the racism they endured.

Housing

Asian house buyers were effectively allocated certain contained geographical areas of towns such as Oldham. In 1988 when the Commission for Racial Equality (CRE) investigated an estate agent in Oldham it found that 'the firm tended to recommend white areas to prospective white purchasers and Asian areas to Asian purchasers, to accept instructions from white vendors to deter prospective Asian purchasers and to offer mortgage facilities only to white clients'.[5] Those Asians who did apply for council housing were hit by racism from the local authority that had an unofficial *policy* of segregation—as the *Oldham Independent Review* into the town's riot found:

> A formal investigation by the CRE into the local authority's housing allocations in 1991 found that the council were discriminating against Asian applicants by segregating them from white households into the centre of town and by placing them into lower quality housing in the Clarkwell and Waterloo Street estates. The council had also failed to review its allocation policy and its ethnic data on households. In 1990 the CRE also found that some estate agents promoted segregationist policies by steering ethnic minority and white residents into different areas; the minority ethnic areas being poorer and ones with already high minority ethnic populations.[6]

Asians who did try and move out geographically were likely to face hostility—as the *Oldham Independent Review* also found: 'We heard from many Asian Oldhamers that they did not seek to live in exclusively Asian surroundings, but that every time they moved into a new street,

white people began to move out, and it is very clear that this phenomenon, popularly known as white flight, has been occurring on a wide
scale'.[7] The *Oldham Independent Review* showed that Asians were also
afraid that hostility and isolation would make them the prey of racists.
They were largely absent from Oldham's housing estates, meaning that
chances of Asian and white families mixing together (as happens in
England's inner cities) were blocked. The 1991 Census showed that a
quarter of the white population of Oldham lived in local authority
housing compared with 13 percent of Bangladeshis and 9 percent of
Pakistanis—and a 1995 housing survey showed there had been no significant change in that balance.[8]

Geographical segregation therefore had little to do with 'self-
segregation', 'the lack of desire of people from white and Asian
backgrounds to live together',[9] or the 'comfort of living with people
whose customs were familiar in an unfamiliar context'.[10] Neither was it
to do with Muslims' desire to 'live close to facilities such as mosques'[11]
or close to 'their' shops—other explanations advanced in the riot reports.

Jobs

Asians in the mill towns suffered high levels of unemployment following
the collapse of Britain's textile industry. Racism in the jobs market has
clearly had the effect of isolating some groups of ethnic minorities—most
noticeably Pakistanis. As a recent authoritative Cabinet Office report on
ethnic minorities and the labour market (commissioned by Tony Blair)
states, 'The decline of the UK textile industry has had far more of an
impact on Pakistanis in the north of the UK than it has had on any other
ethnic minority group'.[12] Where Pakistani workers have tried to get jobs
outside their traditional areas of employment they have met racism. It has
been demonstrated that 'similarly qualified ethnic minority job applicants
were three times less likely to be offered work after a job interview than
white applicants'.[13] As a Pakistani male from the Manchester area told
researchers, 'I was turned down and there was no reason for it as I had the
qualifications, I had the necessary experience. I had a friend, a white guy
who worked in that company and he told me that they had employed
someone white who had less qualifications than me'.[14]

Exclusion from the labour market is so deep that some Asian workers
refer to 'white industries'. In the riot-hit towns one of the biggest sectors of
local employment is the council. Yet the *Oldham Independent Review*
showed that, despite the 1976 Race Relations Act outlawing racism in
jobs, out of 11,621 employees in Oldham Metropolitan Borough Council
only 2.63 percent are recorded as being from the ethnic minorities. The
ethnic minority population of Oldham MBC is 11 percent. The breakdown

is even more revealing—just 74 (out of 11,621) are Bangladeshis (0.65 percent of the workforce), 137 Pakistani (1.18 percent of the workforce), four black Africans, 23 black Caribbeans and six Chinese. None are at senior management level. Only 7.5 percent of the Oldham NHS Trust is from the ethnic minorities.[15]

A measure of the collapse of industry in the mill towns in the north and racism in the job market on a national scale is the astounding figure that one in eight male Pakistani workers is presently employed as a taxi driver or chauffeur and over half of male Bangladeshis work in the restaurant business (compared with the national averages of one in a 100 workers in each trade).[16]

Schools

Despite racist assumptions otherwise, the vast majority of Asian parents wish to have their children educated in mixed schools. One 1997 study found that most Pakistani and Bangladeshi parents either had no preference about the ethnic mix of their child's school or wanted them to be in a school with a balance of pupils from different backgrounds.[17] In fact there was very little difference across all groups including whites, with most people showing no desire to go to separate schools. Yet in Oldham that desire on the part of adults for their children to mix has clearly been undermined. As one ex-teacher put it, after Eastern European and black Caribbean families moved out of the Glodwick area:

> At our school the proportion of children with Pakistani or Bangladeshi backgrounds soon rose to 95 percent, and it was no longer a multicultural school. Many parents were concerned about this, worried that their children were not mixing enough, and that their acquisition of English would be affected. As teachers, we raised these concerns through local politics. We felt that a situation where half a dozen schools had 90 percent-plus children from Asian backgrounds, while the rest were practically all white, was disadvantaging all our children, who needed to grow up learning with and from one another. Our warnings fell on deaf ears, with the result that we now effectively have a segregated education system.[18]

The marketisation of the education system under Tories and New Labour has compounded this situation. One aspect is the creation of under-resourced and declining schools through the operation of league tables. Another factor is the way local education authorities have lost any effective control over where pupils go to school. Now if a white parent does not want their child to go to a particular school for racist reasons then it is allowed under the guise of 'parental choice'.

Language

Much has been said on the ability or otherwise of Pakistanis and Bangladeshis to speak English and the supposed effects of this on their ability to integrate. This is a central argument because it goes to the heart of the notion being pushed by the government and others that if you don't speak sufficient English then you cannot be regarded as having an 'allegiance' to Britain. Of course language is a factor in people's ability to operate in society, but the debate over it has been skewed so as to lay the blame at the door of Asians. Keighley Labour MP Anne Cryer has campaigned against Asians arranging marriages with a partner from the subcontinent. She says that many cannot speak English and therefore are guilty of disadvantaging their children and segregating themselves. Cryer complained in a destructive intervention in the aftermath of the 2001 riots, 'When they [children] go to school they don't have any English, because nearly always there is one partner in the family who doesn't have English…therefore we are having children going to school at four and five without any English. This delays their start to academic life'.[19] Cryer's argument was taken up by Blunkett who said that Asians should be discouraged from arranging marriages with people from the subcontinent.

Yet recent educational research has shown that language is not the *key* determinant to the success or failure of Bangladeshi or Pakistani pupils. Virtually all of those in the school system today were born here and are bilingual rather than monolingual. In any sane society the fact that a child could speak more than one language would be seen as a boon, not a handicap. It is racism that means children who can speak another European language are regarded as high achievers while those who speak Urdu as well as English are seen as backward (this is despite the fact that somewhere around half a billion people globally can speak and understand Urdu).

Ofsted, the schools inspectorate, recently commissioned a definitive study showing that language was not a central explanation for lack of educational achievement. David Gillborn and Heidi Safia Mirza's report pointed out that Pakistanis and Bangladeshis are not the only South Asian group who speak another language at home. The report showed that Indian school pupils who are also bilingual were, as a group, the highest performing of all the South Asian categories. As the report concluded:

> *This is a highly significant pattern. For one thing, the attainment of Indian pupils suggests that having English as an additional language is not an impenetrable barrier to achievement. The most comprehensive survey currently available on this matter suggests that a majority of **all** [my emphasis] British Asians speak a non-European language: 88 percent of Indians, 92 percent of Pakistanis and 97 percent of Bangladeshis. In some British Asian*

*communities there has been a decline in the use of the community languages
between adults and children; about a third of Indians, African Asians, and
Pakistanis normally spoke to younger family members in English.*[20]

Therefore, if speaking another language at home was the key determinant to educational success, Indians would be down at the bottom of the
pile with Bangladeshis.

It is not language, but class and economic position, combined with
effects of racial discrimination and stereotyping, that are the *key* factors
holding Pakistani and Bangladeshi children back. Indeed the level of
Pakistani educational achievement is much more complex than popularly
put. Latest research shows that, 'although at the national level Pakistani
youth are less likely to attain five higher grade GCSEs than their white
peers, this pattern is reversed in some areas'.[21] This disproves the theory
that a homogenous cultural inferiority is innate in Pakistani groupings—
that they are destined to do badly because of *who they are.*

Figures show that, in four out of ten local educational authorities that
monitor by ethnic origin, Pakistani pupils are *more* likely to attain the
benchmark of five higher grade GCSE's than white pupils locally.[22] The
same goes for Bangladeshi school students. Studies show that in the 1980s
these were at the bottom of the educational 'achievement heap', but by the
1990s this had begun to change. In particular inner city areas they had
begun to close the gap with their peers. As Gillborn and Mirza observed,
'Bangladeshi pupils in Tower Hamlets (where a full quarter of the
country's Bangladeshi pupils are educated), were attaining higher average
exam scores than their white peers as early as 1991'.[23] This phenomenon
has since been repeated in other geographical areas. This proves once
again that having an additional language to English, speaking a south
Asian language at home or having parents who may have limited English
has not been the main factor affecting a child's education. The notion of
the 'language disadvantage' of Pakistani and Bangladeshi pupils is a racist
construction. As one educationalist has pointed out, 'Too often bilingual
children are perceived as being merely non-English speakers; they are perceived as a problem'.[24]

Yet the myth of language being at the root of the problem facing
Asians is still widely accepted. The *Oldham Independent Review* insists:

*Parents have a responsibility to ensure that their children start speaking
enough English for lessons to be conducted in English, but this is impossible
at present when many parents do not themselves have enough command of
the language to help their children. This is particularly the case where young
parents have arrived from the subcontinent with no knowledge of English.*[25]

And David Blunkett, citing Asians' supposed resistance to learning

English, has put in his new nationality measures the speaking of English up to test standard as a prerequisite for British citizenship.[26]

As has been pointed out, young rioting Asians had no difficulty in articulating why they were so angry at the racism they were protesting against. As the Cabinet Office report pointed out, 'Lack of language fluency is certainly not a factor in explaining unemployment among young ethnic minority males. High rates of fluency among the young suggest that other factors have a much greater impact on young people's employment opportunities than language'.[27]

'Asian racism'

In the run-up to the northern riots one of the 'facts' pushed by the local and national media and picked up and exploited by the British National Party was that of a wave of 'racist attacks by Asian gangs' on whites. In Oldham the local police chief had been asserting for years that 'racist attacks' on whites outnumbered those on Asians—a situation unique to the whole of the Greater Manchester area. This problem of 'Asian racism' was repeated as fact in the Oldham report into the riot: 'Racism is not just a one way process and there have been many examples of attacks by Asians on whites'.[28]

But closer scrutiny of these much touted figures shows a different phenomenon entirely—one springing out of the general hostility towards the Asian population by those in authority. As authors of a recent in-depth study into racist perpetrators in Oldham say, this definition of Asian racism 'emerged initially with the full authority of the police and was reproduced with little or no critical commentary in the local press. The trend towards white victimisation was then treated as an established fact in the local authority's [1999] crime and disorder audit'.[29]

The researchers found what they termed a 'spiral of media and police perceptions' that effectively forged racist myths into fact. The police exaggeration of Asian 'racism' has been partly helped by the new definition of a racist attack as a result of the Macpherson inquiry into the murder of Stephen Lawrence: 'A racist incident is any incident which is perceived to be racist by the victim or any other person.' The police have clearly used this wide definition—which was intended to force them to take racist attacks seriously—to define racism according to their own prejudices. In addition there is an understandable reluctance from Asians to contact unresponsive and racist police. This has led to an under-reporting of attacks on Asians. As the researchers point out:

> *Perhaps the figures on racist incidents have been produced by a greater readiness on the part of whites than of Asians to report incidents they believe to be*

racially motivated (and willingness to believe this has itself been encouraged by the police and media accounts of the problem since the mid-1990s). It is also likely that Asians...might come to believe that there is no point in reporting incidents to the police, on the grounds that they are likely to be met with disbelief or victim-blaming. The pattern of reporting racist incidents could thus become systematically skewed, with important social effects... The repeated representation of [young Asian men] *as a threat to social order and in particular to innocent whites might also promote fear, suspicion and hatred among sections of the white population—a possibility not lost on far right political groups.*[30]

The most notorious case of skewed reporting was the branding of a street robbery by Asians on Oldham pensioner Walter Chamberlain as 'racist' following its categorisation as such by the police—thus handing the BNP a propaganda coup on a plate. The subsequent trial of the Asian youths involved found that there was no racial motivation to the attack—but by that time the myth had become 'fact'.

Of course there are some examples where Asians, pushed beyond endurance by racism and attacks from whites, and having no recourse to the police, have hit out not just at Nazis or racists, but at wholly innocent white people. But such incidents are rare and should be viewed as a response to the racism Asians face.

The false promise of assimilation

The New Labour government, backed by various reports and think tanks, has responded to the riots and 11 September by demanding the forced assimilation of Asians, asylum seekers and poor migrants. It argues that a combination of tightly controlled immigration of certain groups, the compulsory learning of English, an oath of allegiance to the queen, a period of extended two-year 'probation' for Asians coming here to marry, and so on, will lessen racial tensions. Over time, the argument goes, Asians thus managed will embrace 'British culture' and in crude terms 'be more like us'. This is a domestic reflection of the message that the Western powers are promoting (and enforcing) internationally—that everything else is inferior and must be remade in the image of Western market capitalism.[31]

But does assimilation into the sort of British 'national culture' that Blunkett might want all of us to adhere to automatically lessen racism—especially of the institutional type?

If this were true then black Caribbeans would be a group largely freed from the effects of racism. After all, black Caribbeans nowhere live in black ghettos, they speak English as their first language, they intermarry into the general population, their children mix with white children in integrated schools, and if they have a religion it is most likely to be a branch of Christianity. In short, they have no supposed cultural barriers stopping them becoming part of the mainstream of British life. Yet for all the black newsreaders, fashion designers and artists, athletes, the smattering of black businessmen and politicians, the celebrated contribution of black musicians to popular music and the general level of integration into the working class, the position of most black people in economic terms is no better than it was 50 years ago.

The above-cited Cabinet Office report contradicts much of the racialised ideology pushed by the government that commissioned it. On assimilation the report argues that:

Some research has suggested that groups such as Bangladeshis and Pakistanis have low levels of assimilation…however, assimilation is a blunt tool to measure the social and economic success of groups, as it is prone to counter-examples. Arguably, some groups have low levels of assimilation, but are still prosperous (for example, the London Arab communities), whilst others are well assimilated but still suffer problems [such as black Caribbeans].[32]

The report demonstrates that the assimilationist thrust of government policy not only stokes resentment towards ethnic minority groups, but also lays the blame for racism on the victim.

The Cabinet Office report refers to 'bridging social capital'—in other words, the degree to which a group has the ability to get itself out of social and economic isolation. The government's argument is that Pakistanis and Bangladeshis cannot get out of poverty because they lack the skills (which include the English language and British 'norms') to do so. The argument runs that if they were more assimilated then they could 'bridge the gap'. But, as the Cabinet Office report points out:

While the lack of bridging social capital might perhaps help to explain the large disadvantages for Pakistanis and Bangladeshis, it is not clear how it can explain the fact that disadvantages are also quite large for black Caribbeans, who are socially perhaps the most integrated of all the visible ethnic minorities (as indexed for example by their rates of intermarriage with white people). Chinese relative economic success is also quite hard to explain by this kind of argument.[33]

Economic indicators show that British-born black Caribbeans, arguably even more 'mainstream' than their parents, still suffer institutional racism in the labour market. The Cabinet Office report comments that in the 1970s black Caribbeans were twice as likely as their white peers to be jobless and that 'there is no sign that matters have improved for the second generation in the 1990s: indeed, we find that…in the case of second generation black Caribbeans [and Pakistanis] the unemployment rates were over twice those of the white British men of the same age'.[34]

So black Caribbeans as a group are economically 'down there' with poor Asians, regardless of their differing levels of assimilation.

The 'ethnic penalty'

Racism is deeply embedded in capitalist society. Some commentators in the aftermath of the 2001 riots have crudely reduced racism in housing and jobs purely to economic factors —but what we see in fact is a synthesis and an interaction of the two.

The Cabinet Office report shows that, even after taking out all factors affecting people's employment chances such as educational qualification, training, experience and parental status (all of which themselves may be influenced by the workings of racism), there is still a clear gap in the position of blacks to their white counterparts that can only be explained by racism.

Statisticians call this persistent gap the 'ethnic penalty'. The existence of this penalty challenges the notion that the general lower position of black people in society can be explained by either their culture or their supposed lack of desire to mix with other 'races' (or in the case of young black men their supposed 'ghetto love' of guns and violent rap music). A summary of this research shows that, taking all the variables into account, if a typical man was black rather than white, he would, on average, be 2.5 times more likely to be unemployed. There is a similar gap of 2.38 times between white and black women.[35]

The Cabinet Office study shows that, taking all variables into account:

●*Ethnic minority men are less likely than their white counterparts to secure a professional post... Black men suffer the greatest disadvantage* [black women are at a similar disadvantage].

●*As a group, ethnic minority men on average still have lower average earning power per week than their white peers. For example, Caribbean men have £81 less average earning power per week than their white counterparts.*

●*Among ethnic minorities, black Africans are the most disadvantaged. On average they have £132 per week less earning power than their white peers* [despite having on average higher educational qualifications].[36]

The study concludes that:

●*Ethnic minorities remain disadvantaged in terms of employment and occupational attainment. In fact, when key variables are taken into account, some groups become more disadvantaged.*

●*All ethnic minority men were shown to have a persisting disadvantage in earning power.*[37]

The report points out that 30 years of race relations legislation has not led to an end to institutional racism:

> Racial discrimination and harassment persist today despite the enactment of existing anti-discrimination legislation and measures... Moreover, the evidence suggests that this persisting and changing form of harassment and discrimination has served to block significantly the opportunities of first and second-generation visible ethnic minorities in the labour market. This has inhibited their economic integration into British society, and, arguably, has negatively affected other aspects of the wider integration process.[38]

Racism is not only confined to economic factors. Black people remain the targets of police racism. The number of violent black deaths in custody shows no sign of relenting. Despite the public exposure of racist police stop and searches, they continue at epidemic levels—partly fuelled by New Labour's 'crackdown' on street crime in London. Figures released during the Macpherson inquiry showed that black people were on average five times more likely to be stopped by police than their white counterparts (the figure was even greater in places like Merseyside, and Devon and Cornwall). Although the number of stop and searches dropped following the public outcry after Macpherson, the proportion did not drop for blacks, and indeed went up to the point where they are now seven times more likely to suffer police stops than their white counterparts. As the National Association for the Care and Resettlement of Offenders (NACRO) commented, 'The new figures show...that more and more black people are being stopped by the police, while the number of white people being stopped has declined... The figures...explode the myth that the Stephen Lawrence inquiry has made the police reluctant to stop and search black people'.[39]

Some commentators, especially those close to the police, have argued that there is no racial bias in police stop and searches. Yet even a Home Office study found, after examining the 2000 British Crime Survey, that 'black people were more likely than any other group to be stopped by the police while on foot or in a car'. The report showed that, when it came to car stops, 'after taking other demographic factors into account, being black still remained a predictor of this form of stop, as did being Pakistani or Bangladeshi'.[40]

Are racist attacks on the rise?

Recent polls show that many black people believe racism is getting worse. Institutional racism, highlighted by the Macpherson report, is clearly a major element in this conviction—people are rightly angry at continued police racism, government anti-asylum measures, racism in the labour market and so on. And they are less likely to accept it after Stephen Lawrence. However, when it comes to racist attacks, the picture is contradictory. According to police figures there has been a rapid rise in the reporting and logging of racially motivated incidents since the Lawrence inquiry (a 75 percent increase in reporting between 1998 and 1999). However, the 2000 British Crime Survey, a more accurate measure than police figures, shows *lower* estimated rates of racially motivated offences than in the 1995 survey (280,000 in 2000 against 390,000 in 1995).[41]

It is impossible to tell whether racist attacks are on the increase or not from the figures. What we do know is that racist violence leaps up whenever government or press scares against asylum seekers are whipped up, or when fascist parties gain a foothold in any particular area. Past experience of such scares shows that whenever racism towards asylum seekers is fuelled British-born blacks and Asians also suffer attacks. The suspected killers of Stephen Lawrence were secretly filmed pouring out racist bile against 'immigrants' yet it was a British-born integrated young black man who was murdered. Given this reality, it is a tragedy that some black people articulate deep prejudice against asylum seekers and groups of new immigrants.

Black people and racism in education

One of the deepest expressions of institutional racism affecting black people, and one that has been long documented, is the unequal treatment of their children by the education system. The previously cited Gillborn and Mirza report graphically sketches this downward slide:

> At the start of their compulsory schooling black pupils are the highest attaining of the main ethnic groups in (a particular) LEA, recording a level of success 20 percentage points **above** the average for the authority. At Key Stage 2 [age 10-11] pupils in the same group are attaining **below** the LEA average and in their GCSE [age 16] examinations they attain 21 points below the average. Information such as this raises important issues. That any ethnic group could enter school 20 points in advance of the average but leave 21 points behind opens up an important area for educational debate on ethnic minority attainment.[42]

Recent figures show that the exclusion of black Caribbean pupils still runs at a disproportionate rate. They are still three times more likely to be excluded from primary schools and four times more likely to be excluded from secondary schools than their white counterparts.[43] Some have sought to explain this disparity by advancing the notion that male black Caribbean pupils become alienated from school due to special 'cultural' factors that lead to a turning away from schooling. Gillborn and Mirza refute this:

> Research evidence...challenges such stereotypes about alienation, disen-chantment, and lack of motivation. In comparison with white peers of the same sex and social class background, for example, studies show that black pupils tend to display higher levels of motivation and commitment to educa-tion. This has been documented in relation to pupils' enthusiasm for school, rates of attendance and support for homework.[44]

The focus on the supposed particularities of black Caribbean boys also ignores the fact that black Caribbean girls are also disproportion-ately excluded from school.[45]

Studies also show that black pupils are more likely to get encourage-ment from home to go on to further and higher education. Black Caribbean pupils are motivated, but knocked back by their experiences of the school system. Gillborn and Mirza say that 'a good deal of quali-tative research...argues that black pupils are often treated more harshly (in disciplinary terms) and viewed with lower teacher expectations on the basis of teachers' assumptions about their motivation and ability'.[46]

Again there is an interaction between race and class. Generally speaking pupils from better off families of whatever colour do better than their manual working class counterparts of whatever colour. So working class black Caribbeans find themselves alongside working class white and Pakistani pupils in the lower sets in the school streaming system. Once in a lower set, the more difficult it is to rise, regardless of colour. But again, as in stop and search, this is not the full picture. Such is the racist bias against black Caribbean pupils that the effect of social class difference is much less pronounced than for whites. Gillborn and Mirza argue that in one study 'the data suggest that even when control-ling for social class, there remain significant inequalities of attainment between different ethnic groups. For example, only white pupils improved year on year regardless of their class background. During the research period there were points of relative decline in the attainment of African-Caribbean and Pakistani/Bangladeshi pupils from both manual and non-manual backgrounds'.[47]

Education policies by successive governments are aggravating this situation. Present figures show that black Caribbean pupils are less likely to attain five higher grade GCSE passes than anyone else. This was not always in case: 'In 1988 [the year of the Tory Education Reform Act] black pupils were the most successful of the groups from manual backgrounds. The relative decline of working class black pupils has, therefore, been marked'.[48] Similarly New Labour's 'get tough' policy of allowing schools to exclude children more easily will result in more black Caribbean children being barred from education.

The politics of ethnicity and community

Labour's history of tight control of immigration combined with 'race relations' laws has been the basis of its policies towards black people since the mid-1960s. The overall position of British reformism to race was summed up by Roy Hattersley's 1965 formula: 'Integration without control is impossible, but control without integration is indefensible'. As one commentator has pointed out, Hattersley was 'really arguing that in order to eliminate racism in Britain, it was necessary to practice it at the point of entry into Britain'.[49] Anti-immigration law from the mid-1960s onwards has been accompanied by an extension of race relations legislation, but that black immigration is a 'problem' to be managed remains at the core. The New Labour government has followed this pattern by enacting new anti-asylum measures while simultaneously amending the Race Relations Act.

There has been an intellectual decoupling by which racist attacks are unacceptable—but racist laws are not. The most recent embodiment of this has been Home Office minister Mike O'Brien, who in New Labour's first term could simultaneously be the minister in charge of the Stephen Lawrence inquiry *and* be in charge of steering his government's anti-asylum law through parliament.

The passing of race relations laws has also given governments a lever by which to attempt to influence and incorporate struggles against racism. One of the strategies of the state has been to draw black activists into niches in the system. This is a general strategy employed by capitalism to blunt resistance, but it has taken on a specific form in the arena of race and racism. Each new Race Relations Act and its policy spin-offs have created a layer of professionals whose job has been to police and enforce aspects of legislation. Their funding has largely been dependent upon central government. Whatever the motives of individuals who enter that system, the tendency is for them to bend to pressure from above.

Those at the very top of the profession have consciously been used by those in power to exercise downward control over what has become known as 'the black community' or the 'ethnic minorities'. Under New Labour, especially in the wake of the Macpherson inquiry, this incorporation has accelerated—with the creation of high paid 'race advisers' in various government departments, race advisory committees at the Home Office and Scotland Yard and the handpicking of 'safe pairs of hands' to top jobs such as the leadership of the Commission for Racial Equality.

Black New Labour MPs such as David Lammy have been positioned to 'take on' black 'Old Labour' figures such as Diane Abbott—so in April of this year Lammy argued directly against Abbott in favour of segregated education of asylum seeker children in a House of Commons debate.[50]

The strategy of incorporation has roots in the period of post-war immigration. In 1964 CARD (the Campaign Against Racial Discrimination) was founded to pull together the Labour left, moderate blacks, peace activists and church organisations. CARD was an openly reformist organisation that lobbied for laws against racism.[51] The then Labour government co-opted CARD's leadership to posts on an official advisory committee and successfully stopped CARD campaigning against new anti-immigration laws. CARD collapsed a couple of years later under challenge by the left and black nationalists, but the strategy of state incorporation of groups and individuals continued over the next decade—culminating in 1976 with the creation of the Commission for Racial Equality. The Tories, faced in the 1980s with inner city riots that involved black and white youths, also sought to incorporate black leaderships by handing out money to black organisations.

For more than a decade following the demise of CARD more radical groupings and individuals sought to confront racism, including entering united fronts such as the Anti Nazi League. However, the downturn in workers' struggles both nationally and internationally in the 1980s not only pushed back the general fight against the system but also pushed back the fight against racism. With the downturn there was a fragmentation of the struggle against racism and a reassertion of demands that the system could accommodate. This move away from struggle saw 'black politics' that had sought to unite blacks and Asians under the same banner, replaced by 'ethnic politics' by which various groups sought their 'own identity' distinct from the others. This development was speeded by black separatists who constructed splintered 'identity' politics and hierarchies of oppression.

Black activists were encouraged to enter the Labour Party in order to change it. They pushed for a 'black section' (against hostility from the Labour hierarchy). But some 15 years later not only do we still see a mere handful of 'ethnic minority' MPs and ward councillors (12 MPs in the Commons and 530 councillors out of 21,000 in April 2002) but most of the initial 'rebels' have made their peace with the party and the system—note the antics of Keith Vaz and his links with the billionaire Indian Hinduja brothers, and the transformation of Paul Boateng from civil rights firebrand to enthusiastic backer of authoritarian and anti-immigrant policies.

The limits of multiculturalism

In working class areas 'ethnic' politics saw 'community' leaders begin to argue that not only were they not 'black' (yet 'black' was never a descriptive term—it was always a political one) but they were not 'Asian'—they were Pakistani, or Kashmiri, or Gujerati and so on, and should be negotiated with on a separate basis. In the same way black Caribbeans were encouraged to define themselves apart from Asians and the other groups previously under the 'black' banner. This 'ethnic' ideology ignored the question of class entirely—the one factor that could unite not only blacks and Asians but also working class whites in a common struggle.

The 2000 report 'The Future of Multi-Ethnic Britain', commissioned by the Runnymede Trust and headed by a Labour peer, articulated this fragmented analysis par excellence, when it proclaimed, 'Citizens are not only individuals but also members of particular religious, ethnic, cultural and religious communities... Britain is both a community of citizens and a community of communities, both a liberal and a multicultural society'.[52]

The politics of 'ethnic' fragmentation dovetailed with the state's strategy of incorporation of black leadership and the dividing off of one against the other. The state pushed back anti-racist polices that challenged the system, eradicating them in the first instance from the education system through the Tory Education Reform Act and dismantling bodies such as the Inner London Education Authority (ILEA), alongside the promotion of, or at least toleration of, an official version of 'multiculturalism'. This shift was contested at the time by anti-racist and socialist educators who rightly argued that race could not be delinked from class, whereas the advocates of multiculturalism argued that 'extremism alienates' and that 'there are so many things that *can* be worked for—gently, tactfully and politely'.[53]

As understood by most people multiculturalism is of course a step forward. Aspects of multiculturalism can and do have a role to play in challenging the racist notion that there is one culture—'British'—and that others are either non-existent or at best inferior. This is a widespread feeling in society. In May 2002 a poll carried out by MORI found that 86 percent of people disagreed with the proposition that 'to be truly British you have to be white' (with only 9 percent agreeing), with 78 percent of people agreeing that 'it is important to respect the rights of minority groups'.[54] It is clear here that support for multiculturalism is an expression of basic anti-racism.

However, as a *formal political strategy to defeat racism* multiculturalism has proved to have serious limitations. It has developed into a narrow strategy that seeks to push the state into granting 'space' for ethnic minorities, rather than arguing for radical change of society as a whole. This is not a new idea—in 1967 then Labour home secretary Roy Jenkins rejected what he called the 'flattening' of assimilation for promotion of a policy of 'equal opportunity accompanied by cultural diversity in an atmosphere of mutual tolerance'. The difference was that in the 1960s and 1970s this was a definition rejected by most of those engaged in the fight against racism, but by the 1980s it had re-arisen during a general period of defeat to be embraced by elements of black nationalism and the minority elevated into 'race relations' jobs. It has also been given a philosophical veneer by post-modernist theorists who argued that individuals' identities are so separate that not only is there no shared experience between them but shared communication is barely possible.[55]

This concept, increasingly pushed through the 1980s and 1990s, of different hermetically sealed and static cultures practised by distinct 'ethnic' groups outside any material analysis of society in which people live, has provided ammunition for the right.

The multicultural slogans of 'different but equal', 'tolerance and diversity' and the boiling down of Asian cultural aspects into a national dish, dress or religious practice has allowed the racism of 'separate development' in through the front door. Anti-racism strives to unite black and white against racism and to expose the class relations at work—but it is clear that a type of multiculturalism can be promoted by those who have no intention in challenging racism whatsoever.[56] It could only be a matter of time before opportunists on the right and far right would begin to demand their 'cultural space' and 'rights' in response to multiculturalism.

Thus the BNP argues a 'theory' that apes multiculturalism. Its leadership say the BNP is not racist, but that it merely holds that 'cultures' are separate and incompatible—the English, its argument goes, have a 'natural' need for their culture just as Asians and blacks have theirs. Of course this is a cover for their fascist politics, but nonetheless claims a legitimacy within the official doctrine of 'multiculturalism'. BNP leader Nick Griffin has unfortunately had some success in promoting this idea among blacks themselves—in the spring of 2002 he was invited to write an article on race and culture in a glossy black professional men's magazine, *Untold*.

Yet the idea of separate cultures, which dictate the way in which people view themselves and others around them, is not reflected in reality.

For instance, the government's insistence that Muslims (and future black and Asian immigrants) become more English begs a crucial question: what is this English or British culture we are all supposed to sign up to? A moment's thought shows that there is nothing in common between the 'culture' of the royals or top businessmen or most politicians and the way of life of working people (black and white) in Britain.

Across the world, Britain included, ordinary people's culture is increasingly merging. Culture in its widest sense means the way people live their lives, their social practices, attitudes and sense of the world around them. Culture in artistic terms—works of art, performance, rituals and so on—is the smaller part of people's everyday cultural existence. Globally working class culture tends towards the same reference points. Not only do workers everywhere increasingly wear the same clothes, enjoy the same films and so on, they also have access to the universal political language of anti-capitalism. A growing number of British people identify with an international feeling that the rich have too much power and that governments give in to the powerful. But Blunkett is not encouraging Bangladeshi children or Somali asylum seekers (let alone white children) to embrace this global culture of revolt.

When it comes to fragmentation on ethnic lines the idea of separate cultures makes even less sense. Kashmiris, Gujeratis and Punjabis in Britain (as in the subcontinent) share the vast majority of their cultural outlook. They most likely understand the same languages. They dress similarly, watch the same Bollywood movies and Asian cable TV, and eat the same sorts of food. Their different religious affiliations do not represent a great gulf between them. And when it comes to their white neighbours and workmates, they increasingly share a commonality of outlook and way of life, especially in the inner cities.[57]

Community and class

One of the major areas where the politics of 'ethnicity' have had a divisive effect is in local politics. Ethnic groupings, each represented by a 'community leader' have been encouraged by state policy, for example through local government and 'urban renewal' and 'regeneration' funding policies.

Groups are expected to define themselves as separate communities to bid for little bits of funding for social facilities. Those who fall behind are left out. So, for example, a 1991 study into the Muslim population of Coventry found that local Gujerati leaders felt that 'the attitude of the council is that the Sikh community are powerful, so give them something. If we don't give something to the West Indians, they will fight on the streets, so let's keep them quiet. But they know we are not going to fight'.[58] The report also found that local authority officers tended to 'attribute a cohesiveness to supposed ethnic minority "communities", which they would not expect to find among indigenous whites, and to assume that a small number of "leaders" speak with authority'.[59]

The 'ethnic community' model, with leaders representing their fiefdom, crucially plays down class divisions and tensions. As with the rest of society, there are different class interests involved. In Bradford, for example, even as early as 1981 a study indicated that between 7 and 10 percent of Bradford's Pakistanis were already living in 'the most affluent suburbs or in comfortable semi-detached suburbia'.[60]

Latest figures show that nationally 17 percent of Asians and 11 percent of blacks are in 'higher managerial and professional' jobs,[61] with a similar percentage of both groups also concentrated in the lowest income brackets. Specific groups have done better than others, with 47 percent of Indians deemed to be in the top social class (this compares with a figure of two fifths of whites and black Africans and a quarter of black Caribbeans, Pakistanis and Bangladeshis).[62] But there is also a class division *within* the Indian population—Indians who follow the Muslim religion are over-represented in the lowest income brackets.

Those who have influence in any 'community' to do with their class position or connections can hold back the struggles of the majority. When Asian youth riot, 'community leaders' are invariably found to condemn them and any attacks on property, although they may try and balance this with criticisms of those in authority for fear of being isolated. Under particular circumstances leaderships and organisations may arise to lead struggles against racism and exploitation, to find that they have also to lead a struggle against conservative 'old guard' elements within their own 'community'. The crucial question, as in all conflicts based on class difference, is which wins out to carry their strategy forward.

As much as 'ethnic' communities are divided by class, they may also be divided through place of origin, family groupings and ties, and religion. For example, in 1959 in Bradford there was just one mosque that everyone (mostly male immigrants) attended, but by 1994 there were 30 mosques, each aligned to different national, regional and ideological strands of Islam.[63] This pattern is also true of other religious affiliations in the city. These religious leaders tend to play a conservative role—for example against the freer integration of young men and women across religious and caste affiliations as well as in wider society. To say, therefore, in towns such as Bradford there is one Asian community to be treated as one undifferentiated bloc is to overlook class and other divisions that exist.

Labour's racialised politics

The notion that community leaders only represent 'their kind' has been strengthened by the operation of the Labour Party in local government—which has historically had a paternalistic attitude to black voters and organisations.

The Labour Party has relied on the allegiance of black and Asian voters—not an insignificant factor in many inner city constituencies. A study into voting patterns in the 1997 election that brought New Labour into office found that 88 percent of black Caribbeans, 82 percent of Indians and 80 percent of Pakistanis voted Labour, compared to 46 percent of whites.[64]

Labour has consistently taken its black and Asian supporters for granted—on the one hand, urging Asian members and local councillors to deliver the 'ethnic vote' while stifling any demands for political representation. One commentator writes how, in Birmingham, 'patronage politics went unchallenged by the party while it was used to secure the position of key white politicians but created an outcry when the same patterns were emulated by Asians'.[65]

The overall relationship of the Labour Party with black voters has been 'racialised'—in other words, they have been related to only on the basis of their race. This has manifested itself in various assumptions: that 'ethnic' leaders could deliver mass votes; the suspicion that Asians were motivated by 'takeover' and 'back home' politics; and the placing of its few black parliamentary and council candidates in 'black' or 'ethnic' constituencies where they were assumed to have colour allegiance, regardless of their politics.

In Bradford this policy of dealing in a top-down fashion has inevitably distorted what remains of emasculated local politics. As one study into voting patterns in the town describes:

> The dynamics of the process are as follows: a Kashmiri politician mobilises his kinship network to gain control of a local party ward. When he wins a seat as a Labour councillor, his Kashmiri rival decides to offer himself to the Tories. Clan and caste rivalries are then played out on the streets and bewildered voters wake up to discover that this or that party's safe seat has fallen to the opposition. This has happened every year since 1995 with wards continuing to be suspended... The future Lord Nazir Ahmed was twice victim of such exclusion. In an interview with *Q News* [Muslim youth magazine] after his appointment to the House of Lords, he mentioned that he had first sought parliamentary selection in 1992, only 'to come unstuck at the hands of predominantly Indian Muslim party members who insisted on asserting nationalist rivalries [against himself as a Pakistani/Kashmiri]...in 1997 he tried again, this time in Bradford West, only to be denied by caste factionalism [within the Kashmiri community].[66]

One does not need to have a stake in Lord Ahmed's political career in New Labour to appreciate the destructive nature of the fragmentation of the struggle against racism into 'ethnic' rivalries for local influence.

These divisions also strengthen the idea that 'ethnic minority' councillors deal with the problems of their 'own kind' while white councillors should look after their 'own kind'. As the *Oldham Independent Review* cites, 'We have heard complaints that the council officers tend, in wards where there are both Asian and white councillors, to use the Asian councillors for dealing with problems in the Asian areas and vice versa'.[67]

This was bound to provoke competition between workers on the basis of colour, especially in run down areas, and to provide political space, as we have seen in Burnley and Oldham, for the far right to gain a foothold in local politics.

The roots of racism

Marxists have a unique analysis of racism, its roots and its role in present society. Racism arose at the beginnings of capitalism as a justification for the transatlantic slave trade. Marx in *Capital* precisely located 'the turning of Africa into a warren for the commercial hunting of black skins' in what he caustically termed as 'the rosy dawn of the era of capitalist production'. As historian Eric Williams wrote, 'Slavery was not born of racism: rather racism was the consequence of slavery.' Williams explained that the formation of racist ideology *followed* the establishment of the slave trade:

> *The features of the man, his hair, his colour, his dentifrice, his 'subhuman' characteristics so widely pleaded, were only the later rationalisations to justify a simpler economic fact: that the colonies needed labour and resorted to negro labour because it was the cheapest and the best. The planter would have gone to the moon, if necessary, for labour. Africa was nearer than the moon.*[68]

Racist ideology emerged as a way of overcoming the contradiction of early capitalism that advanced the creed of equality, yet relied for its early accumulation on mass slave labour. The way of overcoming this contradiction was to push Africans down *beneath* the rest of humanity. Thus could Thomas Jefferson write in the American Declaration of Independence of 1776, 'We hold these truths to be self evident, that all men are created equal, that they are endowed by their creator with certain unalienable rights, that among these are life, liberty and the pursuit of happiness,' while at the same time being an owner of slaves.

Part of the consequence of early racism was to drive a wedge between white and black, where previously poor whites transported to the colonies had been regarded by their plantation masters and the upper classes in Britain as on the same level as Africans. So, with the rise of slavery and racism, slaves in tobacco colonies in Virginia were barred from Christian baptism, while white labourers were recoded as 'Christian white servants'. Whites were no longer allowed to have sexual relations with Africans, whereas previously they had mixed freely. As historian Edmund S Morgan argues, this elevation 'placed the white servants psychologically on par with their masters'.[69] It made the poor whites *feel* part of the dominant group, but without improving their economic position in relation to the ruling class. Not only was there the racist construction of a 'black race'—later buttressed by pseudo-scientific theories—but there was also the construction of a 'white race'. This was an early example of racism as a tool of divide and rule.

Although the African slave trade was abolished, racism, lodged as it was in capitalism, expressed itself through the racism of empire—in which subjugated peoples were regarded as 'backward races' that needed European rule as a civilising force. Ideologically it enabled the rulers of the various European empires in Africa and Asia to plunder the colonies at will, while suppressing with the utmost brutality those who fought for their freedom.

However, it would be wrong to think that racism today is merely a hangover from slavery. If that was the case, racism might be eradicated through education combined with 'race relations' laws against its worst manifestations. Marxists, however, argue that modern racism grows out of and is sustained by the material conditions of late capitalism. Its basis lies in economic competition between workers and it has benefits for the ruling class as a weapon that weakens the entire working class. Capitalism, as Marx argued, brings workers together at the point of production, but then pits them against each other. One of the ways in which the ruling class has historically managed this is by stoking resentment between indigenous workers and groups of new workers—immigrants who because of their economic position are often brought in to work for less pay and worse conditions. This is part of the history of the northern English towns, where the mill owners were happy to recruit cheap Asian labour and then segregate them from whites in the workplace. As one account of Asian immigration into Bradford describes, 'Those [Asian immigrants] without formal education, the majority, worked the night shifts in the textile mills. Most were wool combers—a dirty job traditionally done by women—who were excluded by factory legislation from working the night shift'.[70]

This capitalist process has been a constant pattern in Britain and other European countries. Each new group of workers has faced racism, both from racist politicians and explicitly racist parties who have found levels of support among sections of hostile white workers who felt their own precarious economic position threatened.

Conditions in the northern towns show clearly how racism can arise out of the competition for scarce resources. The material basis for racist antagonisms is plain: the report into the riot in Burnley found that 40 percent of the town's homes are dependent on some sort of state benefit, with 42 percent of children reliant on free school meals. Burnley residents' health is worse than the national average, with the town suffering 'high levels of teenage pregnancy, mental illness and increasingly high levels of drug and alcohol misuse'. Four of Burnley's 16 wards are within the worst 20 percent in England when it comes to education and skills levels. Nearly 27 percent of the town's houses are deemed unfit for human habitation, 15 percent are vacant and house prices have fallen so far as to make them virtually unsellable—saddling mortgage payers with huge amounts of negative equity.[71]

It is out of these conditions that the scapegoating of Asians could take hold, compounded as we have seen with segregation and the politics of 'ethnic' divisions.

The nature of racism today

Racism today has fluidity—its immediate focus can shift quickly and is not necessarily defined by colour. For example, racism towards asylum seekers can be aimed at Eastern Europeans as much as at Africans. All the stereotypes and beliefs of inferiority employed in the past against black Caribbeans are now employed against Kosovans. This is partly because globalisation and the collapse of the former Soviet Union have changed the nature of international migration—the poor migrants are not, as they were in the colonial past, exclusively defined by having a differing pigmentation to the indigenous population.

At the same time previous immigrant populations can express prejudice towards new arrivals—so some black Caribbeans do articulate racist stereotypes against West Africans, Eastern Europeans and asylum seekers. Similarly, some ex-immigrants who consider themselves to have 'made it' and identify strongly with 'Britishness' may use the same racist arguments that were once employed against themselves or their parents. In other parts of the world racist stereotyping can express itself outside the lexicon of colour. A modern example is the prejudices whipped up in West Africa at various points between Ghanaians and Nigerians. In 19th century Britain the main focus of racism was Irish immigrants.

However, when racism finds new victims it does not turn away from its original ones. So racist attacks continue to be carried out against easily identifiable targets—people with a dark skin—and, as this article has detailed, the brunt of institutional racism continues to be borne by blacks.

It has been argued that modern racism has an entirely new manifestation, which Tariq Modood has termed 'cultural racism'. Modood says that although 'colour racism is the foundation of racism' there is a separate racism 'which uses cultural difference to vilify or marginalise or demand cultural assimilation'. He argues that this new racism specifically affects religious groups such as Muslims, and demands new measures that fall outside existing anti-racist strategies—namely the extension of race relations legislation to cover Islam.[72] Even setting aside the limitations of pursuing legislation as a strategy to defeat racism, Modood overstates the shifts in the nature of racism. In fact, racism has always employed supposed cultural difference as a cloak for its core thrust. Racism against Jews at the turn of the 20th century had cultural overtones:

> *People of any other nation, after being in England for only a short time, assimilate themselves with the native race and by and by lose nearly all of their foreign trace. But the Jews never do. A Jew is always a Jew.[73]*

The 1965 Labour government openly argued its justification for immigration controls in cultural terms:

> *It must be recognised that the presence in this country of nearly 1 million immigrants from the Commonwealth with different social and cultural backgrounds raises a number of problems and creates various social tensions in those areas where they have concentrated. If we are to avoid the evil of racial strife and if harmonious relations between the races who now form our community are to develop, these problems and tensions must be resolved and removed.[75]*

Again in 1968 Tory MPs argued in favour of controls against Kenyan Asians on cultural lines: 'We cannot overwhelm ourselves with large numbers of people, who, however worthy, are alien, have alien cultures, different temperaments, totally different backgrounds and habits and different ways of life'.[76] Infamously it was Margaret Thatcher who argued in 1978 that Britain was in danger of being swamped by those of a 'different culture'.

Do whites benefit?

Marxists reject the argument that 'all whites are racist', with its implicit assumption that the white working class is somehow fascism's 'natural' constituency. The logic of this belief can have a damaging effect on anti-racist strategy, for example leading to writing off 'white areas' in constituencies where the Nazis are trying to build a base in favour of campaigning exclusively in 'black areas'. This idea of an innate racism in whites gained influence in the 1980s when it formed the basis for 'racial awareness training' (RAT), mainly used in the public sector. RAT was theoretically underpinned by the writings of an American academic, Judith Katz, who believed that racism is 'a psychological disorder...deeply embedded in White people from a very early age on both a conscious and an unconscious level',[76] and that 'being White...implies being racist. White people are responsible for the perpetuation of racism in a White racist system'.[77] Katz's solution was to shift away from a collective response to racism towards confronting individuals, who needed to be 're-educated' out of their racist attitudes. Katz defined racism as an individual psychological 'sickness' afflicting a whole group rather than a product of society. It is significant that RAT's forerunner was HAT—'human awareness training'—developed by the US military during the Vietnam War period to try and mitigate against racism towards black GIs undermining its operational ability.[78]

For Katz's theory to stand up it has to be proved that (i) all whites are racist and (ii) all whites benefit from racism. Yet even a cursory examination reveals many historical and contemporary examples of where white people have fought racism and furthermore have chosen black leaders to represent them in their struggles against the system. For example, historians have now uncovered the extraordinary depth of white working class support in Britain for the abolition of slavery.[79] The civil rights movement in the US had many white activists prepared to go on 'freedom runs' into the Deep South to challenge segregation. The London Chartists chose a black man—William Cuffay—to lead them in the 1840s, and the white workers of Battersea, south London, twice elected an Indian Communist, Shapurji Saklatvala, to represent them in parliament during the 1920s. In recent times the Anti Nazi League has mobilised tens of thousands of white workers and students against the threat of fascism.

Marxists crucially argue that racism is not in the material interests of white workers. The northern mill towns are a good example of how white workers *do not* benefit from racism. Segregation and high levels of 'popular' racism against Asians over decades have created a weakened working class, and brought no benefits to whites (or Asians).

Studies have also shown that, the greater the grip of racism on white workers, the worse their level of exploitation by the ruling class. In the 19th century Marx argued that the antagonism of English workers towards Irish immigrants was 'the secret by which the capitalist class maintains its power'. An American Marxist, Szymanski, looking at the economic position of white workers in the southern states, found that the more racist they were the easier it was for the bosses to exploit them on the basis of an imaginary white solidarity. He concluded that white workers 'appear to actually lose economically from racial discrimination'.[80] Another study in Australia found that white workers lost out because of their racism towards Aborigines: 'Whites on NT [Northern Territory] cattle stations had the lowest wages of any white workers in Australia and worked longer hours without proper overtime "because they allowed the bosses to treat the Aborigines like dogs".'[81]

Conversely, the more solidarity there is between white and black workers, the better off they are collectively—a 1992 CRE study, 'Part of the Union', found that there was a link between greater involvement of black trade union members and effective [trade] union organisation'.[82]

New Labour props open the door

New Labour has declared that it wishes to oppose racism and halt the rise of the far right. But its economic and social policies all flow in the opposite direction. Its racist anti-asylum and immigration policies continue to poison the debate around race and racism, as does its targeting of Muslims. Blair has also set himself against wealth redistribution—the growing gap between those at the top of society and those at the bottom is not of concern to him. But it is the poverty in some areas of Britain that is contributing to a feeling of hopelessness and division that can nourish racism. Oldham is the 38th most deprived local authority in England, yet the town has been 'awarded' a pitiful £211 million in special regeneration funding for the 18-year period 1993 to 2011.[83] As the *Oldham Independent Review* points out, the money that has been allocated to Oldham has been made up of small 'penny packages' of funding which are supposed to 'lift up' geographically small areas. These scraps of funding have to be fought for by local representatives, with 'winners and losers' being the built-in outcome. Racists have latched onto and amplified complaints that 'they' are getting more than us—when 'they' are people of a different skin colour. These myths can take hold, even if they are not true. The *Oldham Independent Review* points out that, in reality, 'rather more than half the funding has gone to areas with low proportions of minority ethnic inhabitants'.[84] Yet not only is the amount of money in *total* pitiful, but the competitive market model imposed by New Labour on every aspect of funding of public services is stoking resentments.

The government says it wants people to integrate, yet the segregation of children is set to widen. The government is committed—in its effort to undermine the comprehensive system—to a 'plurality' of schools, from more private companies being let into education, more specialist schools that pick their pupils, and more religious schools. As has been pointed out in the various riot reports, this drive is disastrous. The Cantle report commissioned by the government found that 'one Church of England school...in the midst of an Asian community had a policy whereby pupils had to produce a letter from their local vicar to prove they and their parents were regular churchgoers. Consequently, Muslim parents rarely bothered to apply to send their children to this school and were effectively excluded from it'.[85] This scenario will multiply as more and more faith schools are established. In a desperate attempt to square the circle, the government is proposing that faith schools should practise 'inclusiveness'—but how can they do this while barring groups of students with the 'wrong' or no religion from the school roll? In a bizarre move the government has picked up on the proposal that schools should practice 'virtual' integration instead, by having religious schools video-conference and internet link with other schools![86]

New Labour's central ideological response to the northern riots has been to concede the main plank of the racists' argument—that divisions among sections of Britain's working class are permanent, and that 'ethnic' boundaries naturally predominate. This is a facet of the crisis of reformism.

Thus New Labour, because it refuses to enact policies that meet social need, argues that the only option open to it is to mediate between different ethnic groups while spreading a general message of 'tolerance'. It follows that for New Labour the problems that exist in towns like Burnley are not to do with poverty and racism, but to do with 'cultural factors'—language, religion, 'self segregation', the 'natural' desire of people to stick to their 'own' and so on. Home Office documents thus argue that segregation is not fundamentally a product of particular economic, political and social factors, but an expression of the desire of 'different ethnic groups' to retreat into 'comfort zones made up of people like themselves'.[87]

This has resulted in the government either giving in to or promoting racist arguments. The response of government environment minister and Oldham MP Michael Meacher to the riots was to utterly concede the BNP case, announcing:

We are not talking at this point about extra money [my emphasis]. *It is important that money which had previously been targeted at a particular area, and which has produced a very strong perception of unfairness—that certain parts of the community are being favoured over others—goes borough wide.*[88]

Home secretary David Blunkett then deliberately opened up a debate on citizenship on the eve of the publication of the various riot reports to deflect away from the deprivation pointed to in the reports, while in the run-up to the May 2002 local elections he used the phrase 'swamping' in connection with asylum seekers in an open bid to tempt racist votes.

In a similar manner racism and deprivation among the black population in the inner cities has been turned on its head, with a focus switched to 'black crime' and supposed violent cultural aberrations among black youth that somehow lead them *to alienate themselves* from the rest of society. Unfortunately this turn away from material explanations towards cultural theorising has been echoed by some black leaders—so, for example, prominent London figure Lee Jasper has called for co-operation with the police against so called 'black on black' violence (revealingly there is no equivalent term 'white on white' violence), while the head of the CRE, Gurbax Singh, has backed more 'stop and search' of inner city blacks.

The basis for unity

The polarisation in British society creates opportunities for the left as it does for the far right. There exists in Britain a large potential for a united class-based fightback that has the struggles against inequality and oppression at its core. There is a revolt in Britain against the politics of globalisation and US imperialism that has produced an internationalism that actively opposes racism and scapegoating. The movement against the war on Afghanistan, followed by demonstrations in defence of the Palestinians, has seen Britain's Muslims take to the streets in a mass political fashion as never before—opening up the possibility of activists, especially the younger generation, allying with the broader movement and joining the ranks of anti-capitalist and far left organisations. Of course religious leaders and small Islamist sects will attempt to keep control over what they regard as their constituency, but this is far from inevitable. Objective circumstances mean that the gap between Britain's Asian population and the wider working class is not as large as it is generally portrayed. In very real terms, most of the Bangladeshi and Pakistani population, for example, are in the ranks of the working class and increasingly integrated with their fellow workers.

The segregation and antagonisms present in British society show only a partial picture. Most people (84 percent) from what are termed 'ethnic minorities' live in the inner cities—just under half live in the Greater London area. The capital is one of the most mixed cities in the world. Nearly a quarter of all Londoners were born outside the UK.[89] Four fifths of Britain's black Africans and three fifths of all Bangladeshis live in London.[90]

These workers have a young age profile in general: 'The ethnic minority population of the UK...is projected to account for more than half of the growth in the working age population over the next ten years'.[91] And over 85 percent of ethnic minority young people stay on in full time education (compared with 67 percent of whites) and therefore mix with other young people from different backgrounds.[92]

There are large variations across different groups, with high levels of employment among black Caribbean and Indian women and low levels among Bangladeshi women. However, in general blacks and Asians are increasingly present in Britain's colleges and workforce, with a greater level of integration present among the young.

Young Asians have a more relaxed attitude to the society they live in than their parents. Even as far back as 1983 some 65 percent of young Asians did not see anything wrong with wearing Western clothes. As one study put it, 'There was...a feeling that girls should be free to wear what they wanted. Others mentioned that clothes were not important and made no difference to cultural traditions.' The main reason for wearing Western clothes was to help them mix in more easily.[93]

The trend for social integration is upwards. Black Caribbeans are the most integrated group socially, with the 1991 census showing that 40 percent of black Caribbean men and one in five black Caribbean women aged 16 to 34 are currently living with a white partner. There are indications that mixed relationships are generally becoming more common, with the 1991 census showing that over half of men and women classified as 'black other' were living with a white partner. The figures also show that 'the proportion of couples who are ethnically mixed is higher among younger couples'.[94]

The 1991 census also found that 7 percent of Indian men and 4 percent of Indian women were living with a white partner. There is little doubt that new census figures, once analysed, will see this figure rise. The trend across all 'ethnic minority' groups, especially in the second generation, is towards mixed relationships. Even among Pakistanis, given the hold of the arranged marriage system, there seems to be a trend (from a low base, as one would expect) towards marrying across 'ethnic' and religious lines. Figures from 1991 show that 5 percent of Pakistani men and 1.2 percent of Pakistani women had white partners. A study has found that 'there appears to be some indication from the detailed analysis of data that inter-ethnic unions are more common among "second generation" Pakistani men'.[95] One would expect this as Pakistanis' general integration into society, especially in the inner cities, continues.

The impetus for more mixed relationships partly lies in changing attitudes of white people towards blacks. A 1996 survey found that '74 percent of whites said they would not mind [if one of their close relatives was to marry an Afro-Caribbean], rising to 88 percent among young people. When it came to Asians, seven out of ten whites said they would not mind, rising to 85 percent among younger people.[96]

This 'everyday' integration exposes the nonsense of exclusive 'ethnic' and 'cultural' groupings. In areas such as inner London it would be more accurate to identify a *common* youth culture drawn from many sources than a number of distinct ones, for example. It is also significant that in the present period fascists have by and large given up on trying to organise in areas such as inner London where there are large mixed populations—preferring to base themselves in outlying areas with relatively few black and Asian people. Surveys show that racist attacks are more likely to happen outside the inner cities. A 2001 survey found that in the previous 12 months 'one in 12 of the ethnic minority population in Northumbria have reported a racist incident...compared with one in 200 in the West Midlands'.[97]

There have been two developments that have put the politics of anti-racism, as opposed to ethnic politics, back on the agenda. The first has been the determination of Asian youth in the northern towns not to be stereotyped as passive and under the control of conservative community leaders. Their taking to the streets to defend their areas from attack by the BNP and their willingness to take on the police show they want to challenge racism, both of the fascist and the institutional kind.

The second has been the campaign for justice for Stephen Lawrence. This has had a deep impact on British society. It exposed the workings of institutional racism, and provoked popular anger at the police. It was public pressure that made the incoming Labour government grant a public inquiry, not the campaign by the *Daily Mail*. This pressure showed itself during the inquiry as people, black and white, showed their solidarity with the family. The willingness of people to sign petitions in support of the Lawrences' demand that Metropolitan Police commissioner Paul Condon should be sacked was as strong in small towns in Scotland as it was in inner London. The main plank of support for the Lawrence campaign came from the trade unions, from collections by individual members and through large donations by the TUC. The Lawrence campaign was seen as a working class cause.

A section of the white population changed their perception of the police during the inquiry. An ICM poll on the eve of the publication of the inquiry report in February 1999 found that one in four people now believed that most police were racist.[98] This attitude shift was partly to do with white working class people's own experience of the police, but also an understanding taught through the inquiry that the police singled out black people for 'special treatment'.

One of the achievements of the Lawrence campaign was to have the concept of 'institutional racism' cited as the main reason for the police's failure. Although the police fought a rearguard action against its inclusion in the report, it was a step forward from the Scarman report into the 1981

Brixton riot that put police racism down to the 'bad apples' theory of individual officers' attitudes. In the wake of the Macpherson inquiry came a whole number of other campaigns—supporting the family of Indian student Ricky Reel who was found drowned after an encounter with racists, and campaigns against deaths in police custody (which united black families such as Roger Sylvester's in Tottenham with the white Harry Stanley family in Hackney). In every town in Britain these campaigns could pack a community hall. These campaigns have fought an uphill struggle—although they rest on the support of the public they rely at the end of the day on the system to deliver justice. However, they may be considered as crucial rallying points towards a wider fightback against racism. Alongside these have run a number of campaigns in defence of asylum seekers and against government policy such as the demeaning voucher system, which leaders like the TGWU's Bill Morris have made into an issue for trade unionists. In the 2001 general election the Tory attempt to play the race card fell largely on barren ground, although since then New Labour has pandered to the racist arguments of the right and far right.

There is no unbridgeable gap between the lives of black and white workers. The left not only has to win white workers to anti-racism *in their own interests* but it has to reveal the commonality of the lives of the class as a whole. Workers of whatever colour or religion are being simultaneously blamed for their own situation and subject to harsher controls under New Labour's social authoritarianism. Curfews, heavier policing and means testing for the urban poor have their racist reflection in new rules of citizenship and demands for forced integration for Muslims and asylum seekers. New Labour's contempt for its working class base extends both to Pakistanis and to their white counterparts in the northern towns.

Under capitalism the great mass of workers have a contradictory consciousness. They can move towards the left and the right. When workers shift to the left and into struggle, ideas and prejudices about other groups of workers are increasingly challenged—but nothing is inevitable about this process. Socialists cannot afford to sit back and wait—especially when the far right is posing a false alternative. In the coming period a principled stand against racism combined with a strategy that unites in action all workers in their common interest will prove to be crucial.

Notes

Thanks to Rahul Patel, Brian Richardson, Charlie Kimber, Molly Mahamdallie, Yuri Prasad and Kevin Ovenden for useful comments on drafts of this article.

Terminology—I have used black Caribbean for those who used to be called Afro-Caribbeans because this is the term now favoured by statisticians. The term 'ethnic minority' is an amorphous term, usually a shorthand for people with a different skin colour, but it can also cover groups such as the Irish and Jews, etc. When I use the term 'black', I use it as a political term (not a descriptive term) to encompass Africans, black

Caribbeans and South Asians. The term Asian covers Bangladeshis, Pakistanis, Indians and those Indians who came here from East Africa and the Caribbean.

1   Quoted in Y Alibai-Brown, *Who Do We Think We Are?* (Allen Lane, 2000), p10.
2   *Oldham Independent Review Report 2002*, p9, www.oldham.gov.uk/oldham together/index.html
3   Muhammad Anwar Centre for Research in Ethnic Studies, 'British Pakistanis: Demographic, Social and Economic Position' (1996), p17.
4   Ibid, p13.
5   N Ginsburg, 'Racism and Housing Concepts and Reality', in P Braham, A Rattansi and R Skellington, *Racism and Anti-Racism: Inequalities, Opportunities and Policies* (Open University, 1997), p119.
6   *Oldham Independent Review Report 2002*, op cit, p16.
7   Ibid, p16.
8   Ibid, p17.
9   Ibid, p16.
10   Ibid, p8.
11   Ibid, p16.
12   Cabinet Office, *Ethnic Minorities and the Labour Market: Interim Analytical Report* (2002), ch 1, p63, www.cabinet-office.gov.uk/innovation/2001/ethnicity/ interim.pdf
13   Ibid, p64.
14   Ibid, p65.
15   *Oldham Independent Review Report 2002*, op cit, p34.
16   Cabinet Office, op cit, p56. The use of psychometric tests that businesses increasingly favour has the effect of barring certain ethnic minority groups. As one psychologist commenting on psychometric tests used by British Rail put it, 'If I designed a system to discriminate against Asians, I could not have done it better.' Ibid, p65.
17   See T Modood and R Berthoud, *Ethnic Minorities in Britain: Diversity and Disadvantage* (Policy Studies Institute, 1997), pp320-322.
18   Commission for Racial Equality, *Connections* (Summer 2001), p12.
19   Anne Cryer quoted 12 July 2001 on BBC *Bradford News*. Cryer et al state that Pakistani and Bangladeshi children are 'underachieving' at school. The term 'underachievement' is a throwback to the prejudiced notion applied to black Caribbean children in the 1950s and 1960s that their 'culture' and 'language difficulties' were stopping them advancing at school, and was used as a justification for putting them in ESN (educationally subnormal) schools. This racist myth was exploded in Bernard Coard's 1970 pamphlet *How the West Indian Child is Made Educationally Subnormal in the British Schools System*. It should also be noted that Cryer has a less than consistent attitude to arranged marriages—she is only against them if they involve a 'Punjabi or Bangladeshi' speaker. Also note that an estimated two thirds of those described as of Pakistani origin were born in the UK. Of those not many were born in Pakistan but bought into the country by their fathers at a very early age and therefore are, for all intent and purposes, 'British', and certainly not 'immigrants' by any stretch of the imagination. Also note that over the past decade the trend for arranged marriages with a partner from abroad has been downwards. For example, in 1993 nationally 250 male fiances and 300 female fiancees from the subcontinent were admitted. In 1995 the figure was 140 male and 250 female. The idea that this tiny figure can have such a debilitating impact on the Pakistani community as claimed by Cryer et al is a nonsense. For more details see M Anwar, *Between Cultures: Continuity and Change in the Lives of Young Asians* (Routledge, 1998), p112.

20   D Gillborn and H S Mirza, *Educational Inequality: Mapping Race, Class and Gender—A Synthesis of Research Evidence* (Ofsted, 2000), p10, www.ofsted.gov.uk/public/docs00/inequality.pdf

21   Ibid, p10.

22   Ibid, p10.

23   Ibid, p11.

24   I Siraj-Blatchford, *The Early Years: Laying the Foundations for Racial Equality* (Trentham, 1995) p46.

25   *Oldham Independent Review Report 2002*, op cit, p 11.

26   It should be noted in contrast to the furore round the Asian 'language problem' that nurses recruited from Spain to work in hospitals in Manchester and the north west in 2001 were robustly defended by the Department of Health after they were criticised in some quarters for having insufficient English to understand medical terms.

27   Cabinet Office report, op cit, p78.

28   *Oldham Independent Review Report 2002*, op cit, p4.

29   L Ray and D Smith, 'Racist Offending, Policing and Community Conflict', (unpublished paper delivered to British Sociological Association Conference, March 2002). Thanks to the authors.

30   Ibid.

31   Blunkett's oath of allegiance or citizenship pledge is as follows: 'I [swear by Almighty God] [do solemnly and sincerely affirm] that, from this time forward, I will give my loyalty and allegiance to Her Majesty the Queen Elizabeth the Second, Her Heirs and Successors and to the United Kingdom. I will respect the rights and freedoms of the United Kingdom. I will uphold its democratic values. I will observe its laws faithfully and fulfil my duties and obligations as a British citizen.' (It would be interesting to find out how many people in Britain would sign up to such monarchical nonsense.)

32   Cabinet Office, op cit, p85.

33   Ibid, p86.

34   Ibid, p50.

35   Ibid, p105. This statistical process is called multivarient regression analysis—crudely, the difference in gross and net rates.

36   Ibid, p107.

37   Ibid, p110.

38   Ibid, p112.

39   NACRO press release, 11 March 2002.

40   Home Office Research Study 223, *Crime, Policing and Justice: the Experience of Ethnic Minorities: Findings from the 2000 British Crime Survey*, p70. The report also found that in 1999 black people were more likely to suffer multiple stops than their white counterparts and that they were more likely to be searched—www.homeoffice.gov.uk/rds/pdfs/hors223.pdf

41   L Ray and D Smith, op cit. There is a huge gap between reporting of racially motivated crimes and prosecutions—only about one in five of those reported even make it to court.

42   Op cit, p16.

43   Ofsted, 'Achievement of Black Caribbean pupils: Good Practice in Secondary Schools' (Ofsted, 2002), www.ofsted.gov.uk/public/docs02/achblackcarib_sec.pdf

44   D Gillborn and H S Mirza, op cit, p12.

45   Ofsted, op cit.

46   D Gillborn and H S Mirza, op cit, p17.

47   Ibid, p20.

48   Ibid, p20. This decline has not only hit black Caribbean boys. Black Caribbean girls attain higher than their male peers, but still lag behind their white counterparts. Ibid, p24.

49   R Miles and A Phizacklea, *White Man's Country: Racism in British Politics* (Pluto, 1984), p57.

50   See *Hansard*, 24 April 2002.

51   See D Banton, *Racial Minorities* (Fontana, 1972), ch 1.

52   'The Future of Multi-Ethnic Britain', *The Parekh Report* (Runnymede Trust/Profile Books, 2000) pix. The report was semi-commissioned by the government.

53   See R Hatcher and J Shallice, 'The Politics of Anti-Racist Education', in *Multiracial Education*, vol, 12 no 1 (1983).

54   *The Voice of Britain: Britain Beyond Rhetoric*, MORI Social Research Institute for the Commission for Racial Equality, May 2002.

55   See N Davidson, 'The Trouble with Ethnicity', *International Socialism* 84 (Autumn 1999).

56   One graphic example of 'official' multiculturalism is a series of recruitment postcards produced by the Metropolitan Police, one of which depicts curry ingredients with the slogan 'Bring your culture to the mix', and another utilising the 'I have a dream' photo of Martin Luther King!

57   For a fuller discussion see A Kundnani, 'The Death of Multiculturalism', in *Race and Class* (April 2002).

58   J Ellis, 'Local Government and Community Needs: A Case Study of Muslims in Coventry', in *New Community*, CRE, vol 17, no 3 (April 1991), p370.

59   Ibid, p359.

60   P Lewis, *Islamic Britain: Religion, Politics and Identity Among British Muslims* (IB Tauris, 1994), p23.

61   Cabinet Office, op cit, p30.

62   Ibid, p57.

63   P Lewis, op cit, p58.

64   S Saggar, *The General Election 1997: Ethnic Minorities and Electoral Politics* (CRE, 1998), p36.

65   K Shukra, *The Changing Pattern of Black Politics in Britain* (Pluto, 1998), p85.

66   P Lewis, *In Between Lord Ahmed and Ali G: Which Future for British Muslims*, Bradford Vision paper no 6, www.bradford2020.com/pride/docs/Section6.doc. In the 1997 general election in Bradford a survey showed that in Bradford West 61 percent of Pakistani voters backed the Tory candidate (Mohammed Riaz) compared with the 35 percent who backed the Labour Party candidate (Marsha Singh). See M Anwar, *Ethic Minorities and the British Electoral System* (Centre for Research in Ethnic Relations, 1998), p20. The Bradford West vote should be compared to the national figure by which 80 percent of Pakistani voters backed Labour in 1997 (S Saggar, op cit, p36).

67   *Oldham Independent Review Report 2002*, op cit, p60.

68   E Williams, *Capitalism and Slavery*, (Andre Deutsch, 1989), p20. It is significant that some of the earliest ideologues of racism were slave owners themselves, such as the Jamaican planter Edward Long.

69   E S Morgan, *American Slavery, American Freedom: The Ordeal of Colonial Virginia* (WW Norton, 1975), p331.

70   P Lewis, op cit, p54.

71   *Burnley Task Force 2002*, pp8-9: www.burnleytaskforce.org.uk

72   T Modood, *Racial Equality: Colour, Culture and Justice* (Commission on Social Justice/IPPR, 1994).

73   *East End Advertiser,* 6 May 1889, quoted in C Holmes, *John Bull's Island: Immigration and British Society 1871-1971* (Macmillan, 1988), p68.

74   R Miles and A Phizacklea, op cit, p54.

75   Ibid, p63. It is ironic that those Labour and the Tories were eager to keep out—Kenyan Asians—are a group now hailed by those in power as an economic success story.

76   J H Katz, *White Awareness Handbook for Anti-Racism Training* (University of Oklahoma Press, 1978), p14.

77   Ibid, p23.

78   See A Sivanandan's trenchant article, 'RAT and the Degradation of Black Struggle', in *Race and Class*, Vol XXVI, no 4 (Spring 1985).

79   See J R Oldfield *Popular Politics and British Anti-Slavery: The Mobilisation of Public Opinion against the Slave Trade 1787-1807* (Frank Cass, 1998).

80   See A Callinicos, *Race and Class* (Bookmarks, 1998), chs 5 and 6.

81   M Armstrong, 'Aborigines: Problems of Race and Class', in R Kuhn and T O'Lincoln, *Class and Conflict in Australia* (Longman, 1996), p67.

82   Findings quoted in Labour Research Department, *Black Workers and the Trade Unions* (June 1993).

83   *Oldham Independent Review Report 2002*, op cit, p53.

84   Ibid.

85   *Community Cohesion: A Report of the Independent Review Team,* chaired by Ted Cantle (Home Office, 2001), p16 www.homeoffice.gov.uk/reu/community_cohesion.pdf

86   Ibid, p35. The debate on faith schools has tended to concentrate on Muslim schools. However, the figures show that these schools are a minority—presently in the state sector there are 4,716 Church of England schools, 2,110 Catholic, 27 Methodist, 32 Jewish, four Muslim, two Sikh and one Greek Orthodox.

87   *Building Cohesive Communities: A Report of the Ministerial Group On Public Order and Community Cohesion* (Home Office, 2001), p12, www.homeoffice.gov.uk/reu/pocc.pdf

88   Michael Meacher quoted in *The Guardian,* 15 June 2001.

89   In *Without Prejudice? Exploring Ethnic Differences in London* (Greater London Authority, 2001), www.london.gov.uk/gla/publications/without_prejudice/without_prejudice1.htm

90   Cabinet Office report, op cit, p21.

91   Ibid, p24.

92   Ibid, ch 4, p72.

93   M Anwar, *Between Cultures,* op cit, ch 9.

94   D Coleman and J Salt (eds) *Ethnicity in the 1991 Census, Demographic Characteristics of the Ethnic Minority Populations* (HMSO, 1996), p199.

95   M Anwar, *Between Cultures,* op cit, p34.

96   IPPR Attitudes to Race Survey, NOP/IPPR, 5 Feb 1997.

97   *The Observer,* 18 February 2001.

98   ICM/*Guardian* poll, *The Guardian,* 9 February 1999.

'The centre cannot hold': fascism, the left and the crisis of French politics

JIM WOLFREYS

The crisis of mainstream politics

The events of 21 April 2002, when the fascist candidate for the French presidency, Jean-Marie Le Pen, won more votes than Socialist prime minister Lionel Jospin, and went through to the second round stand-off against the Gaullist Jacques Chirac, were widely described as an 'earthquake'. Certainly they ripped apart the myth, fuelled for a decade and a half by a smug chorus of politicians, journalists and academics, that France was now a nation in which the conflicts of the past, between left and right, bosses and workers, people and institutions, were over. Jospin and Chirac had just come to the end of a five-year period of 'cohabitation' between a Socialist prime minister and a Gaullist president. The arrangement had once been held up as a shining example of the maturity of French democracy, proof that the politics of consensus now underpinned its institutions. On 21 April the president and the prime minister polled fewer votes between them than the number of abstentions. Nobody has ever become president with a lower first round score than Chirac's paltry 19.8 percent. Jospin's vote, meanwhile, was the lowest score achieved by a Socialist presidential candidate since the party's formation. In the process, the party lost half its manual worker vote. During the 1980s the four principal mainstream parties (the Socialists, Communists, Gaullists and the right wing UDF coalition) consistently won three quarters of the votes. In 2002 they were unable to win half the vote despite the 11 million abstentions, which included 40 percent of young voters. This rounds off a ten year period in which all four major parties have experienced their worst electoral result ever.

The results contained a number of paradoxes. Le Pen's score, when added to the 2.34 percent won by Bruno Mégret's rival far right party, was the highest ever for the extreme right, up nearly a million on the *Front National*'s (FN) 1995 performance. But Le Pen's organisation had gone into the election weaker than at any time over the previous decade, following a major split which had seen Mégret and half the party cadre leave in 1999. No left wing candidate made it to the second round, but the total left vote was more or less on a par with that won by the right. The mainstream right, moreover, lost more votes (4 million) than the mainstream left (1.5 million). And although the campaign was dominated by a traditionally right wing issue, law and order, the Trotskyist left won its highest ever vote, topping 10 percent and winning nearly 3 million votes, over three times more than the French Communist Party (PCF).

The PCF, after five years as a loyal partner in Jospin's 'plural left' government, during the course of which its transport minister Jean-Claude Gayssot had helped ensure that more public industries were privatised than under all of its right wing predecessors put together, received the lowest vote in its history, lower even than the number of spoilt ballots. Having long since lost its standing as the biggest party in France, the organisation is now losing its claim to be a party of any long-term significance at all. Once lambasted by Trotsky as a 'trained donkey with a cargo of patriotism', the PCF's current plight is personified by its inane leader Robert Hue, a meek little social democratic pony. The two main parties of the revolutionary left, *Lutte Ouvrière* (LO) and the *Ligue Communiste Révolutionnaire* (LCR), clearly won support from voters disaffected with the compromises of the left in office. But their score was also a reflection of two important developments in French society over the past decade. The 1990s saw a resurgence of labour militancy on the one hand, and on the other the development of political activism beyond the confines of mainstream parties. Towards the end of the decade both began to fuse with a burgeoning anti-capitalist movement associated with figures like José Bové and groups like Attac. The LO/LCR vote confirms that the new mood opened up by the public sector strikes of December 1995, and the impetus this gave to anti-racism and anti-capitalism, has not dissipated. Indeed, while LO's vote confirmed that a significant number of workers identify the organisation as the most resolute defender of their interests, the performance of Olivier Besancenot for the LCR further underlines the volatility of the present situation. His ability to put forward socialist arguments in terms that resonated with the concerns of anti-capitalist youth meant he was able to win the support of more voters under 25 than either Jospin or Le Pen. That a young Trotskyist postal worker, completely unknown before the campaign, could come from nowhere to win over a million votes is an indication that the new mood is generalising and generating a desire for political alternatives to the mainstream.

The 1990s, however, were also years characterised by job insecurity, long-term unemployment and aggressive management attitudes to sackings and working conditions. 'Precarious' employment—part-time, seasonal or fixed term jobs—became particularly widespread. Between 1990 and 1998 the proportion of contracts issued on this basis doubled from 10 percent to 20 percent. By 1998 over 900,000 workers were on fixed term contracts and over 600,000 in temporary posts. In industry, and in the catering, clothing and building trades, 'precarious' work has become particularly widespread. At the Peugeot-Sochaux plant, for example, one quarter of the workforce—4,700 people—are on temporary contracts,[1] while at the Renault-Douai factory the proportion is nearly half—2,000 of the 4,500 workers. The effect of all this has been to increase workers' sense of insecurity, despite the much trumpeted fall in unemployment under Jospin. By the end of the 1990s almost a third of all workers felt that their jobs were in danger.[2] Moreover, as we shall see below, one of the effects of the introduction of the 35-hour week by the Jospin government was to intensify this sense of insecurity. If from the mid-1990s a reaction against this situation began to gather pace, the conditions which gave rise to the reaction have not disappeared.

This situation impacted on the election campaign in various ways. Huge numbers of workers rejected the parties of government. Those at the LU biscuit factory in Calais, furious at the Socialists' decision to stand by and let the owners, Danone, close it down, made plans to spoil their ballots in what they thought would be a Chirac/Jospin second round. Some of them drew up ballot papers printed with a message to Jospin: 'The P'tits LU of Calais thank you for your failure to render assistance against the stock market sackings by Danone of which they are the victims'.[3] *Lutte Ouvrière*'s candidate, Arlette Laguiller, campaigned for companies in the black to be banned from making redundancies. Many of her best attended meetings in provincial France were in areas where LO had few roots but where local populations had been affected by sackings. When it came to the vote, LO and the LCR won 13.5 percent of manual workers' votes, the majority going to Laguiller (despite a concerted campaign against her by the plural left), against only 5.3 percent for the PCF. Although this election saw a dramatic rise in support for the revolutionary left, and the continuing decline in working class support for the Socialist Party (PS) and PCF, Le

Pen continues to win votes from workers and from almost a third of the unemployed. This needs putting into perspective. According to the sociologist Emmanuel Todd:

> It is important to note that on 21 April there was no rise in Le Pen's vote among workers, or only a tiny rise. The real breakthrough took place between 1988 and 1995, when Le Pen went from 16 percent to 27 percent among the working class electorate. Today the figure, depending on the polls, stands at between 16 percent and 30 percent... No, the new phenomenon in 2002, in popular areas, is the rise in the far left and the aspirations that expresses... In effect the Le Pen vote represents a corruption of workers by the values of inequality which ravage capitalist society... The middle classes'...scorn for the people has reverberated among workers against immigrants. The vote for the far left is the rediscovery of the values of equality.[4]

The FN is a party led by a millionaire. It has an essentially neo-liberal economic programme. Studies have shown that its core voters identify with racist ideas and an extreme right ideology and generally enjoy a good standard of living.[5] During the 1980s and 1990s, as the mainstream parties lost credibility, the organisation's promise of change began to attract significant support among workers. The FN's two biggest electoral constituencies are therefore among workers and small businessmen (artisans, traders, petty entrepreneurs)—two groups with opposite interests. What unites them is a sense that things are getting worse, that immigrants are to blame for this, and that radical change is necessary. This has led many to assume that the cause of the FN vote can be located in relation to the presence of immigrants. New Labour's Peter Hain, for instance, referring to the 'intolerable situation' around the Sangatte camp near the Channel Tunnel, remarked that, 'Le Pen did very well in the Sangatte area. If you look at Le Pen's vote it's concentrated right round the border, the German border as well; it's a really disturbing fear of outsiders'.[6] The obvious question to ask would be why it took them, and so many other people in the Nord-Pas-de-Calais region (a traditionally left wing area) until 2002 to realise that there was a border on their doorstep. Hain's arguments are dealt with in more detail below. A more plausible reason for workers looking towards Le Pen's desperate alternative lies with the shortcomings of the Jospin government. One unemployed former PCF voter in Calais gave this explanation for voting FN: 'I can't trust Robert Hue, mixed up in this government and the plural left. Left or right, I've not seen the difference as far as I'm concerned. If I chose Le Pen, it's because he's the only one to be able to shake up all these numbskulls. Lots of those sacked at LU voted like me. It's our chance to kick up a stink'.[7]

Le Pen's score, however, although disturbingly high, was not a reflection of a fundamental shift to the right in French society, or an indication that France is on the verge of fascism. The unrelenting wave of anti-fascist demonstrations which swept France from the moment the results were announced bears this out. The vote for the far right was rather a product of an ongoing process of polarisation, to the left and right, which is squeezing the mainstream parties. These parties are increasingly seen as interchangeable, sharing a consensus on social and economic policy and a commitment to European integration. Invited to compare Jospin's programme, launched on the slogan *'Je m'engage'* ('I commit myself'), and Chirac's, launched on the slogan *'Mon engagement pour la France'* ('My commitment to France') , three quarters of the electorate could see no difference between them. Public indifference was a feature of the first round campaign. Occasionally the mutual contempt which characterises the relationship between population and politicians came to the surface. Chirac was spat at in Mantes-la-Jolie and Jospin squirted with ketchup by two women in Lille ('We wanted to put some red into his campaign'). In Strasbourg the UDF candidate slapped a child who appeared to be picking his pocket.

Widespread disregard for mainstream politicians, reflected in the vote, is fuelled by their corruption, the most corrupt of all being the president himself. Between December 1992 and July 1995, just after his June election on a promise to heal France's 'social fracture', Chirac and his entourage spent around a quarter of a million pounds on holidays, entirely paid for in cash. Chirac and his wife also made sure that measures introduced to keep rents on social housing down were applied to their opulent Paris apartment, situated within walking distance of the Left Bank squat which Chirac visited during the 1995 campaign in a show of solidarity with the homeless. His political allies showed similar enterprise. Chirac's first prime minister, Alain Juppé, was accused of personally intervening to reduce the rent paid by his son on another municipal property. Deputy mayor of Paris Jean Tibéri used public money to pay his son's rent and do the flat up nicely in marble. By this time the existence of the so-called *'système Chirac'*, set up during his time as mayor of Paris (1977-1995), had been an open secret for years. Every year an estimated £2.5 million would be paid to the RPR, via intermediaries appointed by Chirac, in exchange for lucrative contracts from the city's public housing budget. Up to £10 million a year would also be raised from public funds for the RPR by bogus posts for party functionaries.

Sleaze is one of the defining characteristics of mainstream political life. All the major parties are involved to varying degrees in forms of corruption. One of the more grotesque aspects of their current obsession with juvenile delinquence in urban areas is the fact that the maintenance budget for secondary schools in the Paris region is believed to have been used during the 1990s by all four major parties to raise £5.6 million in illegal commissions from companies seeking construction and renovation contracts.[8]

Those seeking explanations for Jospin's failure to take advantage of the constant stream of revelations about Chirac's larceny need therefore look no further than his own entourage. His political fixer, Jean-Christophe Cambadélis, and finance minister, Dominique Strauss-Kahn, were both obliged to drop out of politics for prolonged periods following accusations of involvement in a scam involving phantom jobs for cronies. Laurent Fabius, rehabilitated as a senior figure in the PS, will forever be remembered as the man responsible for infecting part of France's haemophiliac population with HIV-contaminated blood, even if the courts, like some Socialists, considered him 'responsible but not guilty'.[9] One of the many examples of the extent of the degeneration of the PS is the attitude of the so-called *Gauche Socialiste* (Socialist left), which has spent the past couple of years seeking alliances with Henri Emmanuelli, newly rehabilitated himself after being banned from public office and given a suspended prison sentence in 1995 for his part in overseeing the Socialists' Urba slush fund, also based on exploiting political control over public works contracts. Various attempts by the Socialist deputy Arnaud Montebourg to change the law to enable a standing president to stand trial have been rejected by the party leadership. This is partly because the PS plays an active role in the political establishment's vast money laundering operation, but also because the Socialists fear any challenge to the institutions of the republic. Jospin's own desire to be 'statesmanlike' in turn explains his right wing campaign and disastrous claim that his programme was not Socialist but 'a synthesis of what is necessary today'.[10] 'We're not talking enough about workers,' one leading Socialist warned him towards the end of the campaign. 'We have to reassure our social base'.[11] Jospin's last-ditch attempts to effect a 'social turn', like the latest rediscovery of social democratic values by the post-Jospin leadership, are all too little too late.

Beyond the failings of Jospin's government, and the errors of his campaign, is a much more profound crisis. The presidential election result expresses a rejection not just of France's mainstream parties but of the institutions they inhabit. As soon as the election was over, voices from within the mainstream, notably the Green candidate Noël Mamère and the Socialist deputy Montebourg, began to question the viability of the Fifth Republic itself. Established in 1958 by de Gaulle, its institutions were designed to overcome the weakness and instability of the Fourth Republic which had begun to crumble during the Algerian war of independence. Today both president and government stand accused of failing to provide solutions to the havoc wreaked by modern capitalism. A constant refrain of disaffected voters was their contempt for the self satisfaction of a political elite which has done nothing to improve their lives. As a consequence barely half of France's 41 million registered voters were prepared to support candidates with links to the mainstream, with around 21 million people either abstaining, spoiling their ballots or voting for the far left or far right. As one respected constitutional commentator put it:

> France is not alone in experiencing a crisis of politics and institutions which, in the heterogeneous forms of populist nationalism, is surfacing across Europe. But France is not as well armed as others to confront it. Its institutions are damaged. Its parties, which have always been weaker than anywhere else, have been obliterated or are becoming extinct... France is in the grip of a gigantic maelstrom of complex changes which are redistributing profits and losses without anyone being able to provide adequate solutions... New political perspectives for the French and new instruments to embody them remain to be invented. A vast programme, of which not a single element can for the moment be seen on the horizon.[12]

Anger at the apparent impotence of the state is expressed in various forms. Some condemn Jospin's passivity faced with factory closures or the employers' offensive over the 35-hour week. Others seek scapegoats in refugees and demand the state intervenes to clamp down on asylum seekers. Some seek more repression to eradicate crime. Lack of faith in the centre to provide answers has led to the multiplication of candidates. Some, like Jospin's former interior minister Jean-Pierre Chevènement, who combines nationalist anti-globalisation rhetoric with a reactionary record on crime and immigration, want to return to a time when the republican state exercised more authority. Others, like the hunting and fishing candidate Jean Saint-Josse, want to return to a time when rural France was left to its own devices. Neither has a structured party behind them. The *Front National*, in contrast, does. But although Le Pen's score underlines the extreme right's ability to build a stable electoral base feeding off fear and demoralisation, it has yet to transform this into an anchored mass movement of the far right. This was underlined by its comparatively low profile during the presidential campaign, its lack of street sales, its failure to mobilise any more than one fifth of the expected 100,000 supporters for its May Day parade and the fact that it managed to hold only one poorly attended election rally between the two rounds of the election. In this sense, then, the 3 million votes for the revolutionary left, up 1.5 million since 1995, compared to a rise of under 1 million for the extreme right, stand out as the reflection of an active social force, the electoral expression of a genuine, tangible movement of workers and anti-capitalist youth. But if it is true that the left, despite Le Pen's score, is still in the ascendancy, the volatility of the present situation means that there is no guarantee this will remain the case.

If, following the public sector strikes of 1995, there was a 'whiff of pre-1968' in the air, today the atmosphere is more like 1934.[13] Despite differences of scale and intensity, France today, as in the 1930s, is a country of tired and declining institutions, a corrupt political establishment and a centre ground showing signs of buckling under the pressure of increasing polarisation. There exists an unprecedented crisis of all four major ideological currents in mainstream French politics: Gaullism, neo-liberalism, Communism and social democracy. Their failure to offer coherent leadership in a world of growing inequalities, political volatility and war is the context both of the revolutionary left's success and of the resurgent threat of fascism. The FN, like the far right in 1934, is not about to take power and does not yet have a mass activist base. But how serious is the threat it poses? Can Le Pen be stopped? Will a viable left alternative to social democracy emerge? The rest of this article will attempt to address these questions. We begin with an account of how a fascist current around Le Pen was able to adapt the heritage of inter-war fascism to modern conditions, and an analysis of the strategy followed by the *Front National* since its formation in 1972. Reasons will be offered for the revival of the organisation since 1999, and for Jospin's failure, along with an assessment of the decisions now confronting those forces emerging to the left of the Socialist and Communist parties.

Le Pen and the rebirth of French fascism

Le Pen's success represented the high point of a career dedicated to the rebuilding of a fascist party in France in the decades that followed the defeat of the Vichy regime. The key to this reconstruction was a recognition that modern fascism would have to adapt to the post-war period. The quest for respectability was crucial. Le Pen, elected France's youngest ever deputy as part of Pierre Poujade's petty bourgeois populist movement in 1956, was well placed to lend an aura of legitimacy to the fragments of the far right which united to form the *Front National* in 1972. But his career has always been about far more than simply making his mark on mainstream politics. Typical of Le Pen's relationship to the mainstream was his experience as a Poujadiste. Divisions soon emerged between Poujade and Le Pen, who wanted to turn Poujadism into something other than just a movement of shopkeeper revolt. According to Poujade, 'Le Pen was the Trojan horse who tried, at the time, to turn the

Poujadist mass into the great people's party of the extreme right. He didn't succeed and he left us'.[14] In September 1956, when Poujade sacked Le Pen from the presidency of the movement's youth wing, which under his leadership had become a rallying point for fascist activists, Le Pen took six months' leave from parliament and signed up to fight in Algeria. Here Le Pen was to prove himself capable of the most deplorable acts.

This is an extract from the police report of an incident involving a young Algerian which took place in March 1957 in the Villa Susini:

> ...two electric wires were attached to his earlobes and Lieutenant Le Pen himself cranked up the magneto, with the help of which he sent electrical discharges into his body. In the presence of the same officer, young Yagiaoui was hit with a truncheon and was tied, naked, to a bench, feet and wrists bound, and forcibly made to swallow a certain amount of water. Finally, he was confined for five days in an empty hole, dug like a grave in the ground, closed in by barbed wire.[15]

The police commissioner's text ends with the statement, 'Lieutenant Le Pen is a deputy in the National Assembly'.[16] Various other accounts of Le Pen's atrocities have been published over the years.[17] Another surfaced between the two rounds of this year's presidential election. It told the story of the execution of Ahmed Moulay through the eyes of his son, Mohammed Chefif, then a 12 year old boy. Moulay was taken, naked, by French paratroopers and tortured in front of his children, their mother and her four month old baby. Le Pen asked the questions. The paratroopers forced Moulay to drink litre after litre of soapy water. Then they stuffed a towel in his mouth while one of them jumped up and down on his distended stomach. Each time they took the towel out of his mouth he vomited. Then they administered electric shocks. The children listened to the screaming until the ordeal ended with a burst of machine-gun fire. Mohammed Cherif still owns the knife he later found when the soldiers left, with Le Pen's name and division inscribed on the sheath.[18]

On his return to France Le Pen was perfectly frank about his involvement in such atrocities: 'I've got nothing to hide. I tortured because it was necessary'.[19] The defeat of France at the hands of the Algerian National Liberation Front (FLN) and the collapse of the *Algérie française* movement to keep Algeria French provoked a crisis for the far right. 'We put so much hope into this *Algérie française*,' Le Pen later recalled. 'We would have made a national revolution there, to mould new, different men.' He nevertheless refused to sanction the attempted coup of April 1961, not because he disagreed with the methods of the putschists, but because he found their aim of handing French Algeria to

De Gaulle, who didn't want it, 'incoherent and moronic'. [20]

During the 1960s the French extreme right tried to come to terms with three factors to which post-war fascism had to adapt. The defeat of the pro-Nazi Vichy regime, rapid economic modernisation and decolonisation raised the question of fascism's relevance. A former leader of the Vichy militia in northern France, François Gaucher, wrote a book on the subject in 1961. *Le Fascisme est-il actuel?* argued that fascism was characterised by its flexible approach to dogma. This meant that fascists were not obliged to operate in the same way as during the inter-war period. The integration of both the peasantry and the working class into post-war society via urbanisation, industrialisation and the welfare state, along with the emergence of a new middle class whose interests were tied to an expanding state bureaucracy, meant that fascism could no longer simply pose as a way out of extreme economic hardship, as a bastion against Communism or as the defender of old traditions. The experience of fascism in power would also work against any movement that tried to revive it. The far right could no longer hark back to the inter-war period, call itself fascist or retain its previous political programme, some aspects of which were no longer relevant, whereas others 'had proved rather unfortunate when put to the test'. Fascists should aim to mobilise both those seeking tougher democratic government and supporters of an authoritarian state. [21]

Le Pen was no stranger to these ideas. On his return from Algeria he set up a record publishing operation, the SERP, with three associates. One of them later became FN treasurer. Another, Léon Gaultier, had been a member of the Vichy regime and was a former Waffen SS officer. Nazism, for Gaultier, was 'a great altruistic adventure'. [22] With Le Pen and company he produced records like *Songs of the German Revolution: The Men and Events of the Third Reich.* The record's sleeve stated that, 'Adolf Hitler and the National Socialist Party's rise to power was characterised by a powerful mass movement, by and large popular and democratic, since its triumph followed legitimate elections, circumstances generally forgotten.' Gaultier was a friend of François Gaucher's and used to make sure that Le Pen read his work. 'We had the same intellectual tastes,' he said of Le Pen in 1990. 'He was ten years younger than me and I said to myself: he'll carry the torch, he'll carry the torch very well. He hasn't disappointed me!' [23]

Another who shared these intellectual tastes was Dominique Venner, son of a member of Jacques Doriot's *Parti Populaire Français*, which became France's largest fascist party between the wars and openly embraced Nazi rule during the occupation. Venner, like Gaucher, focused on the increasing sophistication of the modern state apparatus and the need for fascism to adapt to contemporary conditions. The struggle over Algeria had shown that the more conservative, respectable elements of the far right could help create a climate favourable to the hard-core, fascist elements, but that they were incapable of transforming popular revolt into revolution. On the other hand, those who simply hankered after Nazi rule were incapable of understanding the demands which the present situation imposed on them. If fascists were to win sections of the state bureaucracy to revolution, they would have to prove themselves capable of running a modern state. In 1965 Le Pen invited Venner's group *Europe-Action* to participate in his latest attempt to play a role as a federator of conservative and hard-core elements, which Poujade had put a stop to a decade earlier. Le Pen took charge of the presidential campaign of Pétain's former information minister, Jean-Louis Tixier Vignancour. Le Pen's efforts were derailed by the charges brought against him during the campaign as an apologist for war crimes (as a consequence of the SERP record mentioned above). He was later found guilty, fined and given a two-year suspended sentence.

The formation of the *Front National*

Le Pen's big chance came in 1972 when the *Front National* was formed. The initiative was taken by the leading organisation on the extreme right at the time, *Ordre Nouveau* (New Order), which believed Venner's analysis of the prospects for modern fascism to be the equivalent of Lenin's *What is to be Done?* The changing role of the state was again central to the analysis of the prospects for fascism. Mussolini's triumph, *Ordre Nouveau* argued, had been due in part to the extreme weakness of the Italian state which enabled the Blackshirts to win over a large part of the state administration and to enjoy almost open support in ruling circles. The modern French state was far more powerful. Movements driven simply by their own spontaneity were unable to go beyond the narrow demands of a particular professional group. No one had predicted the Poujadist movement of 1956, the peasant revolts of 1961 or the student unrest of 1968. The potential for future explosions remained, struggles based around nationalist issues, the workers' movement or the independent professions. Without organisation, however, such revolts would end in defeat. 'No revolution without theory',[24] proclaimed *Ordre Nouveau*.

Every aspect of *Ordre Nouveau*'s activity must therefore be geared towards offering a credible alternative to the regime. This would take time and require flexibility. The far right therefore needed both a hard core of revolutionary cadre able to offer leadership to the movement and wider layers of support in order to expand 'the scope of nationalist struggle by opening out as broadly as possible'.[25] Elections were considered 'an excellent instrument of struggle for a revolutionary party... It is not the form of activity, but the goal which characterises a revolutionary organisation.[26] The means are solely dependent on circumstances'.[27] If they were to escape isolation, violence and revenge attacks on the left must be avoided. At the same time, however:

> ...we have not yet trained our supporters to assert themselves on the streets in large scale demonstrations, authorised or not, and that is very important: it is not enough that they attend our meetings. We must show our strength outside, make our views on various problems heard in the streets, other than by the mere presence of our militants, show our numbers and our determination. In this way our supporters rediscover the taste for militant activity and for combat, and the isolation of our activists is avoided. A revolutionary party is inconceivable without large scale demonstrations.[28]

The conscious use of rallies and marches in developing a fascist cadre was directly inspired by Hitler's *Mein Kampf*:

> The mass meeting is necessary if only for the reason that in it the individual, who in becoming an adherent of a new movement feels lonely and is easily seized with the fear of being alone, receives for the first time the picture of a greater community, something that has a strengthening and an encouraging effect on most people... If he steps for the first time out of his small workshop or out of the big enterprise, in which he feels very small, into the mass meeting and is now surrounded by thousands and thousands of people with the same conviction...he himself succumbs to the magic influence of what we call mass suggestion.[29]

Those who founded the FN wanted a highly organised, hierarchical, nationalist movement with a mass base dedicated to smashing democracy and the left. At the same time they recognised the advantages of a front which united right wing conservatives and fascists.[30] *Ordre Nouveau* reassured its members about the road it had embarked upon:

> The electoral road is not a game. It is not an easy road, but it's the only one which offers the hope of ending up with something serious, which can give our ideas a chance to influence reality... But we shall be all the better armed to follow this route if the demand for honour, for loyalty, and this revolutionary will that makes us the nationalists that we are, remain present in us.[31]

Initital municipal electoral results were poor. In 1973 the FN managed only 1.3 percent of the total poll. The following year doubts were raised about the decision to make immigration the extreme right's central propaganda theme. Despite opposition to immigrants among the

French, it was argued, this had not yet developed into a political attitude, as the election results demonstrated. In some areas of Marseille up to a quarter of the population were immigrants, but the far right had failed to break through even though the local *Ordre Nouveau* branch had been agitating around the issue for four years. The conclusion was that it had been a 'political error' to wage the campaign. Potential sympathisers were scared off, 'traumatised by the issue of racism'.[32] Le Pen found himself under pressure from activists impatient at the lack of success electoralism was bringing.

The election campaign had highlighted the lack of any sort of structure enabling the FN to capitalise on its desire to broaden its activist base. The man Le Pen appointed to address this problem had ample experience of building fascist organisations. Victor Barthelémy left the Communist Party and joined Doriot's *Parti Populaire Français* in November 1936, becoming general secretary in 1939. Under the occupation he was part of an alliance of collaborationist groups which sought to form a single fascist party. A member of the Legion of French Volunteers against Bolshevism, which fought in defence of a Nazi Europe, he was sent on a mission to Italy in 1944 where he worked alongside Mussolini. The other key figure in building the FN was François Duprat. A leading member of *Ordre Nouveau* and proponent of the front strategy, Duprat recognised the need to avoid being openly associated with fascism: 'to be accused of fascism today leads, in many cases, to being excluded from the system, not to say all significant public activity'.[33] This did not prevent him from editing a number of publications dedicated to charting the history of fascism and the fortunes of the contemporary far right. Nor did it prevent him from becoming one of a handful of negationists propogating Holocaust revisionist texts active in France during the 1970s. When he was killed by a car bomb in 1978 Le Pen's newspaper paid tribute to this aspect of Duprat's activities, saluting his attempts to challenge 'all these taboos inherited from the Second World War'.[34] Duprat became a hero for the *Front National*. 'Know that in any case you did not die in vain,' declared the FN's newspaper, 'because we will take up the torch. Your work will be continued!'[35]

The official image cultivated by Le Pen played down these associations. 'I do not define the *Front National* as a movement of the extreme right,' was his message. 'I challenge anyone to find, either in its methods or in its philosophy or in its writings, anything which is extremist. It is a party which professes to be part of the social, popular and national right and which is proud to declare itself on the right. It does not intend to be labelled extreme right'.[36] Duprat, who organised the FN campaign for the municipal elections of March 1977, understood the importance of electoral success: '[A] good result for Le Pen would not only benefit his FN, but all the national movements, who would gain a new political credibility in the eyes of public opinion'.[37] After the *Front*'s electoral breakthrough, Duprat still played a role in binding the FN's semi-respectable elements to the hard core. Every year, on the anniversary of his death, Le Pen insists on taking a group of leading FN members to his grave to pay homage to the man responsible for translating *Did Six Million Really Die?* and whose own publications sought to 'rediscover the very essence of the fascist phenomenon'.[38]

Le Pen continued to urge activists frustrated by the constraints of legality to respect the leadership's strategy and not to be drawn into the orbit of fascist groups which opposed it:

> We know that the legal road imposes great patience. That's why it repels certain young people who then find themselves trapped by...bodies whose principal activity is to attack the FN... These unfortunates do not see that they are playing into the hands of the political police, to the delight of the left and the government. They are lured by the carnival fascism of these little groups only to be crushed by disappointment in the end.[39]

Such groups were condemned for needlessly provoking the government. At the same time other far right groups were attacked for pandering to the mainstream right. There was only one road leading to the overthrow of the establishment parties—that chosen by the *Front National*: 'It is not paved with gold and does not allow us to go very fast... But it's the only one which leads to the true liberation of the homeland'.[40]

Immigration and the rise of the *Front National*

During the 1980s the FN made its electoral breakthrough and began to recruit large numbers of activists and cadre from the parties of the mainstream right. They, in turn, were to bring much greater sophistication to the organisation's programme and propaganda.[41] The catalyst for the organisation's transformation from an insignificant grouping to a major force in French politics was the emergence of immigration as the central issue in mainstream political debate following the Socialist election victory of 1981. There was nothing inevitable about the emergence of this issue or in the rise of the FN. The immigration 'problem' did not fall from the sky—it was relentlessly promoted as a political issue by the *Front National*, aided by the mainstream parties, not unhappy to see scapegoats emerge for the recession which led the Socialists to ditch their manifesto pledges and implement austerity measures from 1982. This played into the FN's hands.

Signs that disaffection with the Socialist government were beginning to benefit the FN began to emerge in the early 1980s. In September 1982, three months after the government's first austerity measures were introduced, the FN organised the most successful event in its ten year history, with over 34,000 people attending its festival. A year later the FN general secretary, Jean-Pierre Stirbois, became deputy mayor of the dormitory town of Dreux after campaigning on the slogan '2 million unemployed are 2 million immigrants too many'. Stirbois owed his success to two things. Firstly, the Socialist Party nationally chose not to confront the main plank of the FN programme, the assertion that immigration and unemployment were linked. The PS candidate in Dreux, who attempted to challenge the FN line, later admitted to being isolated in a party which chose not to distribute any of the literature it had prepared to combat racist ideas, and which in Marseille ran a campaign which flirted with racism. The Socialist response to FN claims that Muslim agitators were behind the strikes taking place in the car industry was to echo the attacks on 'religious and political groups' who did not understand 'French social realities'.[42] (In August 1984 the Socialist government, supposedly in tune with these realities, was to adopt the Dalle plan for the car industry which would entail the loss of between 50,000 and 70,000 jobs.)[43] The second factor behind the FN breakthrough was the decision by the mainstream right to do a deal with the FN and invite its candidates onto a joint slate for the Dreux election. Jacques Chirac, having first rejected such alliances on the grounds that members of the FN had a 'congenital defect', namely racism,[44] now argued that such an alliance with the FN was better than inviting Communist ministers into government.

This set the tone for the next 20 years, during which time the FN made steady electoral progress while the mainstream parties fell over themselves in echoing the rhetoric and programme of the far right. Legislation by governments of right and left over two decades, whether cracking down on asylum and revising nationality laws, or tightening border controls, restricting family regroupment and increasing police powers to carry out identity checks, had a twofold effect. Those wanting to fight racism were increasingly put on the defensive, while the FN gained in strength. Its strategy was constantly to up the stakes in an attempt to make it acceptable to say the unacceptable. A good example of the success of this strategy is a speech made in the summer of 1991:

Our problem is not the foreigners, it's that there's an overdose. It's perhaps true that there are no more foreigners than before the war, but they're not the same and that makes a difference. Certainly, having the Spaniards, Poles and Portuguese working here poses fewer problems than having Muslims or blacks... How do you expect the French worker who lives in the Goutte d'Or and who works with his wife and who, between them, earn around 15,000 francs and who has, on the same floor, next to his council flat, crammed in, a family with the head of the household, three or four wives and 20 kids, and who earns 50,000 francs in social security payments, naturally without working... If you add to that the noise and the smell, well! The French worker on the same floor is driven mad and we must understand him.[45]

This speech was made by Jacques Chirac to members of his party in June 1991. It followed President Mitterrand's decision to embrace what had hitherto been a right wing concept of a 'level of tolerance' of immigration. This, he claimed in 1989, had now been reached. In the same vein his prime minister, Edith Cresson, went on national television to declare that her Socialist government would charter planes whenever necessary to deport illegal immigrants. Former president Valéry Giscard d'Estaing pitched in with the word 'invasion' to describe immigration to France, while his colleague Michel Poniatowski claimed France resembled an 'African boulevard'.

What effect did this 'get tough' approach to immigration have on the *Front*? The organisation's swift and effective response was to show that when it came to racism, nobody did it better than the FN. In November 1991 party chairman Bruno Mégret denounced the threat posed to 'races' by 'generalised cross-breeding'. He then proposed a draconian 50 point plan of immigration measures. These included proposals to legalise discrimination against immigrants in favour of French nationals in housing and employment. Quotas of immigrant children would be imposed on schools and their parents made to pay fees if they wanted the French state to educate their offspring. Immigrants would be denied access to certain basic social security payments including family allowance. The building of mosques would be banned, anti-racist legislation repealed and companies charged for employing immigrants. 'Cosmopolitan references' would be censored from schoolbooks. Nationality legislation would be revised and based on parentage rather than residency. Retrospective legislation, for the first time since Vichy, would be applied to all cases of French citizenship granted to immigrants since 1974. 'Ethnic ghettos' would be 'dismantled'.

The response of the mainstream? A month later the Socialist government implemented point 46 of Mégret's plan, setting up detention centres for asylum seekers. In future, Mégret asked, would government policy take its lead from Vichy? And so the dance went on. When the right returned to power in 1993 the targeting of France's immigrant population formed the centrepiece of its legislative programme. Identity checks, the revision of nationality laws, further border controls—a whole series of racist measures collectively known as the Pasqua laws, many of them taken from Mégret's 50-point plan, were introduced. In the summer of 1996 Chirac's prime minister, Alain Juppé, opted to deal with the issue of the *'sans papiers'*, immigrants without residence papers, many of whom had been rendered 'illegal' by the Pasqua laws. Their plight became a *cause célèbre* and their occupation of the Saint Bernard church in central Paris a focus for a resurgent anti-racist movement. Juppé sent riot police to hack their way into the church with axes. Teargas was used on the children sheltering with their parents inside as the church was forcibly evacuated. Le Pen seized the moment to make public his belief in racial inequality. In turn interior minister Jean-Louis Debré decided to revive measures first introduced under Vichy requiring anyone offering hospitality to immigrants to inform the relevant authorities of their movements.

By the spring of 1998 the FN was in a position to conclude regional electoral alliances with the mainstream right. Leading figures in the French employers' association urged alliances between the mainstream right and the FN; 15 years after its first electoral success, the FN looked to be on the verge of becoming France's third political force.

The lesson of the FN's rise is abundantly clear. The refusal of mainstream parties to contest the FN agenda, and their policy of echoing both its rhetoric and programme, utterly failed to stem the growth of the organisation. By the mid-1990s the FN had 11 MEPs, nearly 1,300 regional and municipal councillors and control of four towns. It won 15 percent of the vote in the 1995 presidential and 1997 parliamentary elections. Whenever immigration dominated public debate the FN vote rose and enabled Le Pen, once a fringe candidate of no significance, to declare himself at the centre of political debate.

When the FN made its first electoral breakthrough in 1983 Giscard d'Estaing concluded that 'now the problem which is the root cause of the extreme right's upsurge must be dealt with: immigration'.[46] This has essentially been the reaction of mainstream politicians and commentators throughout Europe when confronted with the rise of the far right. But what, apart from the far right's insistence on the issue, led people to believe that immigration was the cause of their success? The first analyses of the FN vote in France attempted to show a correlation between the presence of immigrants and support for the FN. One academic even came up with an equation to show a mathematically proven link between the proportion of immigrants in a given area and the size of the FN vote, which would rise and fall depending on the number of immigrants nearby.[47] Later studies proved this was nonsense. One analysis of the FN vote in Paris between 1984 and 1986 exploded the myth of a causal link between immigration and the vote for the far right. In 1984 the FN won a significant share of the vote in the west of the city. In 1986 its vote was highest in the north-east of Paris. Both areas had a high concentration of immigrants, thus feeding the belief that this was behind the vote. All very logical, until a closer look revealed that the immigrant population of western Paris was predominantly Spanish and Portuguese. Was the electorate of the well-to-do 16th *arrondissement* casting a protest vote in the 1984 European elections against the presence of Portuguese gardeners and Spanish concierges? Far more likely was the possibility that these were right wing voters turning to Le Pen out of dissatisfaction with the pro-Europe campaign of the centre-right candidate who led the united right wing slate. Likewise, did it really take voters in the north-east of Paris until 1986 to realise that there was a substantial North African population living in their midst? Far more likely was the possibility that a section of the area's working class electorate was turning to the FN out of frustration with the experience of the left in government.

More convincing correlations could be found between the FN vote and poor housing or economic deprivation. But why did studies focus on immigration in the first place? They did so because academics and the media, faced with the insistent line from the FN and the mainstream parties that there was an immigration 'problem', and confronted with FN voters who listed immigration as their highest priority when choosing a candidate, made uncritical assumptions based on such views. As one outstanding study of voting patterns put it, the decision to focus on immigration, rather than any number of other factors which would correlate with the FN vote, such as the proportion of illegitimate births in 1911 or average summer temperatures, only served to give credibility to the FN line that immigration was the central problem facing French society.[48] The straightforward and much more plausible explanation for the FN vote, that individuals from diverse backgrounds, frustrated at unemployment, falling living standards, economic insecurity and blocked social mobility, were finding a scapegoat for these problems in France's immigrant population, was largely ignored. In a period when the credibility of traditional right wing and social democratic parties was declining under the impact of political corruption on the one hand, and the blurring of the left/right divide due to the emerging consensus over a neo-liberal agenda on the other, capitulation to the FN's themes only boosted the organisation's standing as an alternative to the mainstream.

The immigration issue is politically constructed as part of a process of scapegoating. How otherwise can we explain the situation in a city like Marseille, where the proportion of immigrants in the city's population did not change dramatically between the 1970s and 1980s, but where the electorate, immune to anti-immigrant propaganda in 1973, has voted in disproportionately high numbers for the FN since 1984? In this context David Blunkett's remarks in the wake of Le Pen's 2002 vote, just prior to the election of three BNP councillors in Burnley, about the 'swamping' of schools by the children of asylum seekers, are particularly sordid. The same can be said of Peter Hain's decision to cross the line dividing the soft left from soft racism, announced via a *Guardian* interview about the inability of Muslims to become fully integrated in society. The intellectual colossus providing theoretical succour for such outbursts, Anthony Giddens, greeted news of the far right's resurgence with a call for policies which are 'tough on immigration, but tough on the causes of hostility to immigrants'. A useful translation of this kind of disingenuous nonsense can be found in Alisdair Beaton's *The Little Book of New Labour Bollocks:* 'In order to discourage unreasonable and intolerant people, we are going to become unreasonable and intolerant.' Twenty years of the FN on the rise shows it just doesn't work.

The FN strategy breaks down

Two things were necessary for fascism to achieve success in the post-war period. Firstly, it required a credible and structured organisation which could house the diverse, often competing, tendencies of the far right. Secondly, it required an environment in which its ideas could prosper. The experience of the mid-1980s to the mid-1990s proved that if neither the FN nor its ideas were opposed effectively and consistently, the organisation would grow. The experience of the mid- to late 1990s, however, was to prove that resolute opposition to the FN could tear the organisation apart. Two developments turned the situation around. Firstly the explosion of class struggle of November-December 1995, when millions demonstrated in support of striking public sector workers, transformed French politics and society. The solidarity and confidence generated by the strikes saw the mood of bitter demoralisation which had accompanied the FN's rise begin to dissipate. There was, in particular, a change in attitudes towards the immigration question. This had two important consequences. Firstly, the scapegoating of immigrants began to be challenged. The *sans papiers*, for example, won a majority of public support for their campaign. Secondly, faced with the lamentable failure of either the Socialists or the Communists to take a principled stand against the racist drift in politics, combined with the right's anti-immigrant offensive from 1993, anti-racists, led by two new organisations, the *Manifeste contre le Front National* and *Ras l'Front* began to wage a more combative and confrontational campaign against the FN.

The impact of the anti-racist revival on the FN has already been discussed in this journal.[49] The split which it helped bring about in the FN can be summarised as follows. The effect of the resurgence of labour militancy from 1995 and the subsequent shift in attitudes to racism hampered the FN's ability to set the agenda. These developments, along with an anti-FN

offensive which specifically targeted the organisation, brought the contradictory tendencies that made up the FN into focus and into conflict with
each other. The result was a crisis of leadership. This went beyond a question of personalities. The debate tended to focus on strategic differences. Le
Pen stressed the need for the FN to remain an anti-establishment force,
Mégret argued that alliances with the traditional right would allow the FN
to eliminate its weakest elements. This was partly a reflection of the FN's
twin quest for respectability within liberal democracy, and its desire to
smash that democracy. One of the consequences of the FN's success had
been to intensify the tension between these two aims. We have already seen
that the organisation had around 1,500 elected representatives by the mid-
1990s. Between 1995 and 1997 the party's annual budget had risen from
£8.6 million to £14.5 million. The number of full-time party functionaries
rose to nearly 100 and expenditure on salaries rose from £7.8 million to
£17.8 million.[50] Since 1980 its membership had also increased from under
1,000 to as many as 40,000. Electoral success created the potential for the
bureaucratisation of a large layer of the organisation's cadre and generated
a culture of managerialism which was at odds with the more anti-system
attitudes of much of the membership.[51] Le Pen consciously attempted to
combat bureaucratisation. He insisted that anyone elected on an FN ticket
must pay a sizeable proportion of their salary to the organisation. When the
FN won control of three towns in 1995 some in the organisation argued that
this was a chance for the FN to prove its credentials as a party of government. Le Pen insisted that FN mayors implement the party policy of
'national preference'. Mégret shared the same outlook as Le Pen but knew
he could count on the support of party cadre who saw him as the most likely
to be able to deliver the short term electoral gains which alliances with the
mainstream would guarantee. (This despite the fact that the architect of the
electoral agreements of spring 1998 had been the Le Pen loyalist Bruno
Gollnisch.) Le Pen likewise won the backing of activists suspicious of
Mégret's background as a Gaullist and the danger of 'parliamentarisation'
he appeared to represent.

These tensions, kept in check when the FN was on the up, were
stretched to breaking point by the anti-racist backlash. Mégret was
expelled at the end of 1998 and the organisation split soon after. Le Pen,
until now the unassailable leader of the FN, now found the cult of leadership around him beginning to disintegrate. Revelations began to
emerge about the corrupt and dictatorial way he had led the party.
Further embarrassment came when a newspaper printed a report drawn
up and circulated (by a Megrétiste member of the FN's *bureau politique*) on Le Pen's state of mind following a meeting with a Parisian
psychiatrist:

He [Doctor Grandpierre] *does not find the diagnoses of senile paranoia offered by numerous doctors very convincing... Le Pen is affected not by a psychosis (illness) but by a neurosis (handicap)... Jean-Marie Le Pen is a clinically very pure example of a subject affected by a failure complex. The failure complex means the subject, consciously or otherwise (usually unconsciously), provokes his own failure through fear of the insurmountable responsibilities which too great a success would engender... The handicap has affective origins, and it is all the more uncontrollable by the subject as it is unconscious. That does not prevent Jean-Marie Le Pen from brilliantly playing a role as an orator in opposition without real responsibilities... His mental handicap renders him incapable of leading a very large organisation in a rational manner.*[52]

The split weakened the whole of the extreme right. A significant proportion of FN cadre left Le Pen to join Mégret, including one of his own daughters, the editor of the FN newspaper, over 50 district federation secretaries, the head of the organisation's security force, half the FN's regional councillors, and many of those responsible for drawing up the FN programme over the previous decade. Much of the skinhead fringe also went with Mégret. But Mégret's organisation, denied state funding, had serious financial problems. He was forced to request reinstatement in his former post as a civil servant. The far right press was also affected. One weekly magazine went bankrupt, another halved its number of pages, while the FN newspaper experienced serious financial difficulties. When Le Pen spoke to a rally of FN members in April 1999 he chose the song adopted in the 1998 World Cup by the French football team, Gloria Gaynor's 'I Will Survive', to accompany his appearance on the platform. Le Pen might have thought he was being clever. But a few months earlier he was addressing thousands of supporters to the grandiloquent sounds of Verdi's *Nabucco*. The sight of him speaking to an ageing crowd of faithful cronies to the tune of a kitsch disco anthem spoke volumes for the state of his organisation, particularly when he went on to beg those present each to lend the FN £500 to help it out of its financial difficulties.[53]

The crisis of the FN was underlined later that year. In the European elections Mégret lost his deposit and the FN score fell below 6 percent, although the far right vote as a whole bore comparison with previous scores. Exit polls revealed that the electorate as a whole considered immigration to be the least significant of all issues influencing their choice of candidate. When the FN came to discuss its programme in the autumn the confusion into which the new situation had thrown the organisation was revealed by the attempt by Le Pen's son-in-law to convince the membership that it needed to recognise that France was a multi-faith society and that people could be Muslim and French. Debates were also aired the following spring about whether the organisation should continue to advocate the mass repatriation of immigrants or call for a ban on abortion.

Such episodes are an indication of the turmoil experienced by the far right in 1999-2000. Had the anti-racist mobilisations continued no doubt this turmoil would have intensified, but they did not. The *Manifeste contre le Front National*, linked to the Socialist Party but for a time one of the most dynamic of France's anti-racist groups, decided that the FN was finished, that the *Manifeste* had therefore become obsolete itself and should fold. This gave Le Pen a breathing space. In repairing the damage to the organisation he remained faithful to the strategy outlined by *Ordre Nouveau* 30 years earlier. On the one hand, he strove to bind the membership together, organising a series of dinner debates, activist meetings and rallies across France. He also sent out very clear messages to those who had remained with the FN, reminding them that the role of the FN was not confined to electoralism: 'The national right will be called to power like firefighters or paramedics, when there's nobody else around. It's probably our mission'.[54] When he was suspended from seeking public office after attacking a Socialist Party candidate he gave an interview with *Le Parisien* in which he told how he had been responsible for breaking the far right from its long-held belief that power would be won via a coup d'état: 'I said, "There is no other useful, efficient and legitimate means of winning power than the democratic route."' Now, however, he was bitter: 'I'm aware that the democratic route that I've always followed and advocated has led to us being boxed in'.[55] At the same time he attempted to regain the organisation's legitimacy all over again, recruiting De Gaulle's grandson from the traditional right to play a leading role in the party's European election campaign, toning down his attacks on immigrants and Jews and unveiling a 50-point plan of law and order measures in the spring of 1999.

The crisis of social democracy

The issue of security, or law and order, was to play a major part in the FN's revival. But, like the immigration issue, it did not fall from the sky. When they were elected in June 1997 the Socialists claimed to have three priorities: jobs, health and education. Three weeks after their victory, when Jospin introduced his programme to the new parliament, these had been reduced to two: jobs and law and order, at that time fifth in the list of voter priorities, behind unemployment, poverty, heath and road accidents. It has been largely thanks to the Socialists' constant focus on the issue that law and order is at the centre of political debate.

What linked the left's part in creating the immigration issue in the 1980s and its attempt to push security up the political agenda after

Jospin's election was that both issues were used to detract from the left's failure to deliver social reform. Those who elected Jospin in 1997 wanted to see a reduction in the working week and an end to long-term unemployment and job insecurity. The main plank of Jospin's reform programme was the reduction of the working week to 35 hours. This, it was promised, would create jobs and give people more time to do other things. The reality proved a bitter disappointment for many workers. It is estimated that by 2004 the 35-hour week will have created around 400,000 jobs. But those who feel they have benefited from the reform are generally those who were better off in the first place: middle managers, technicians, qualified (male) workers, and those working in big companies. Their long working days have not changed, but they now get more days off. Those who do not feel they have benefited are manual workers, many of whom have had to accept a wage freeze and the scrapping of overtime payments. Often their workload has increased and they no longer feel in control of their time. One of the principal effects of the reform has been to allow employers to impose flexibility on workers, creating irregular working patterns and the sense that work time is increasingly eating into private time. The variance in the implementation of the reform for different groups of workers, and the growing tendency to draw up working schedules on an individual basis, has increased inequalities between groups of workers and potential antagonisms between individuals.[56] As one Citroën worker remarked after Jospin's defeat:

The 35 hours have swindled everyone. The 35 hours gave too many advantages to management; it aggravated exploitation. Me, I've worked here for over 30 years so I'm not going to start slagging it off. But before, when I worked on Saturdays I got a bonus. Now they're always asking me to work at the weekend, and I get nothing.[57]

Jospin's problem was not simply that his claim to want a 'market economy but not a market society' proved illusory. He also had to do something about it. In this light, the insistence on the problem of 'urban violence' by his government, as Loïc Wacquant has underlined, has little to do with any new developments concerning juvenile delinquence. What is at stake is a redefinition of the role of the state:

A Keynesian state, vector of solidarity, whose role was to thwart the cycles and ravages of the market, to ensure collective 'well-being' and reduce inequalities, is succeeded by a Darwinist state which makes a fetish of competition and celebrates individual responsibility, whose flipside is collective irresponsibility, and which withdraws into its hypertrophied regal functions of maintaining order.[58]

The left coalition's refusal to intervene to stop the closure of the Renault-Vilvarde factory in Belgium immediately after its election in 1997 or the 7,500 job losses announced by Michelin in September 1999 is an indication of this shift. One woman affected by the LU closure in Calais summed up the mood:

> *I always voted Jospin or Socialist before the restructuring plan. For me, it's normal: socialism has always defended the worker. This I've not understood. When Danone said they were closing Calais, the government dumped us. That's why I voted for Madame Laguiller, mostly to put Jospin in the shit.*[59]

Interviewed on television about Michelin's sackings, planned over three years despite a 17.3 percent rise in the company's profits, Jospin was blunt: 'I do not think we can administer the economy.' In one sentence he turned his back on the Socialists' electoral promises to step in when such situations arose. It was down to the unions to do something about it.[60]

Where the state could play a role was in ensuring that law and order prevailed. Jospin and his interior minister, Jean-Pierre Chevènement, along with the former left winger turned security adviser Julien Dray, repeatedly tried to convince the left that law and order was a republican issue, that 'insecurity was also an inequality'.[61] Security, argued Chevènement, was a left wing concept because the Declaration of the Rights of Man put 'safety' on a par with liberty. In the same breath he provided a concrete example of how these rights were to be applied by the Socialists: the entire basis upon which post-war France had dealt with juvenile delinquency, emphasising education rather than repression, was to be turned on its head. Chevènement's republican wish was that children who committed crimes would now be rounded up and locked away.[62]

Trotsky was full of scorn for the attitude of the Radical party in 1930s France, faced with the big bourgeoisie's attempts to cower it with the threat of fascism: 'If you do not stop flirting with the socialists and coyly promising the people mountains and miracles, I will call in the fascists!... After which the Radical camel gets down on his four knees. There is nothing else he can do'.[63] Jospin's defeat, his clearly shell-shocked state as he announced his withdrawal from politics on 21 April, evoked sympathy in some quarters. Leading the tributes was the *Financial Times*, which saw tragedy in his 'leaving the stage like Shakespeare's King Lear—"a man more sinned against than sinning".' What was Jospin's great achievement? Naturally, the 35-hour week was mentioned, but not in the context of any significant improvement it had brought to the lives of the Socialists' electorate. No, as far as the *Financial Times* was concerned the measure instead 'provided a convenient smokescreen behind which more pragmatic policies, such as privatisation, could be introduced'.[64] This was a fitting epitaph to Jospin's political career. It had taken off when, as Socialist Party secretary, he had reconciled the membership to the abandonment of its reform programme of 1981 in favour of austerity measures, and now it had ended with him impotent in the face of a market economy running roughshod over society. In different circumstances and with different results, he found that like Salvador Allende in Chile his government was enduring 'all of the disadvantages of capitalism, but none of the advantages of socialism'.[65] Unlike Allende, however, there was nothing tragic in Jospin's fate. He had not been forced to his knees by the threat of fascism or by a military coup. His desire for 'balance', as one critique put it, 'required other interests—those of the world of work—to be taken into account'.[66] Over time, as workers at Michelin and LU were to learn, 'balance' ceased to mean anything. As the slogan from May 1968 put it, 'To give way a little is to capitulate a lot'. The sorry figure cut by Jospin on 21 April evoked less Shakespeare's Lear than Trotsky's camel.

Anti-capitalism and the revolutionary left

Despite Le Pen's success the situation in France today is vastly different to that which accompanied the FN's initial rise to prominence. Although, as we have seen, two decades of neo-liberal attacks have left their mark on sections of French society, the demoralisation and bitterness of the 1980s have given way to renewed combativity and confidence. The tremendous wave of anti-fascist demonstrations which took place on a daily basis nationwide from the moment the presidential results were announced on 21 April 2002 represented the biggest wave of protests to hit France since 1995. On May Day 2002 around 3 million marched across France, with huge demonstrations not just in Paris, Marseille (100,000) or Lyon, where 50,000 marched in torrential rain, but also in many smaller towns—Perpignan (15,000), Caen (35,000), Rennes (20,000) and Clermont-Ferrand (20,000)—which experienced their biggest demonstrations since 1968 and at the same time experienced something of Seattle, Genoa and Barcelona.

The demonstrations mixed anger, humour, solemnity and irreverence and were characterised above all by their verve and spontaneity. Schools, universities, workplaces, housing estates, associations and trade unions held meetings and mobilised for the protests. Thousands turned up with slogans written on anything they could find: bits of cardboard, pieces of carpet, old sheets and scraps of paper. 'Vote for the crook not the fascist', 'I'd rather be screwed by Chirac than raped by Le Pen', 'You don't discuss cookery with cannibals', 'Zero tolerance for fascists'. Students were particularly active, with entire schools turning up to march. In Paris a group of young demonstrators went into the streets to protest on the night of Sunday 21 April. The following evening they bumped into each other at another demonstration at the Place de la République. By Wednesday's protest at the Bastille they were calling themselves the '*Mouvement spontané du peuple*' (Spontaneous movement of the people) and writing the name on placards and banners. By the Friday afternoon they were meeting up with activists from the DAL homeless association to organise a street forum and drawing up leaflets to hand out to school students with the independent SUD trade union.[67] This was a pattern repeated all over the country. Small groups of people threw themselves into the movement against Le Pen and found themselves joining up with others and suddenly addressing issues which went far beyond the question of the FN. This is not an inward looking, defensive reaction against fascism but a vigorous, confident movement which is spontaneously seeking political alternatives. It is this movement which is posing the question of unity on the revolutionary left and the possibility of building a new anti-capitalist organisation.

Such mobilisations underline the extent to which things have changed since the 1980s. But they have also changed since 21 April. In August 1998 the fear of being co-opted by a political party led to a public statement by representatives of many of the groups associated with the so-called 'social movement'. Their appeal 'for the autonomy of the social movement' declared that the movement would strive for a society based on solidarity and equality through action which bypassed political parties. Since then, however, groups and associations which set out with a deliberately narrow focus have found themselves confronted with questions that require a much more general response and a much broader base from which to act. Groups organising homeless or unemployed workers, for example, find themselves drawn into anti-fascist activity with groups like *Ras l'Front*, alongside other associations like the AIDS awareness group Act-Up or Attac. The Attac leadership in turn finds itself called upon by its associations to draw up a response to events like the presidential election or finds it position on the war on terror challenged by more radical sections of the membership. This means, on the one hand, that autonomy is not really feasible, and on the other that that associations like Attac are not just actors in struggles, they are also themselves arenas where the shape and direction of these struggles will to a certain extent be determined.[68] The experience of Attac is a good example of how the crisis of social democracy is opening up a space for groups and associations which exist somewhere between the status of an association and a political party. Increasingly, however, Attac is being forced to confront situations which can only truly be resolved through the application of the general politics and strategic orientation of a party. Under pressure from the right, which would prefer Attac to operate in the orbit of mainstream parties as a pressure group, and from the left, which would like to see it engage more decisively in the struggle against capitalism, fascism and war, the organisation is prey to paralysis. Its ability to play a full role either in mobilising for anti-capitalist protests, for example in Genoa or Barcelona, or in building an anti-war movement has already been put to the test (with the association found wanting) and is likely to come under further strain.

The thirst for political solutions generated by 21 April is likely to accentuate this tendency. All political parties have experienced a huge demand for membership since the election. This is an expression of the growing understanding of the need for political solutions. All this, then, places an even greater responsibility on the parties of the far left.

All this then, places an even greater responsibility on the parties of the far left, *Lutte Ouvrière* and the *Ligue Communiste Révolutionnaire* (LCR). The two organisations have until now adopted different perspectives. LO's primary focus has always been on building in the workplace. This means it has been able to play an active part in a number of important strikes over the years, but LO has never played a leading role in the struggle against the FN and has refused to engage with the anti-capitalist movement on the pretext that it wants to 'file the nails of finance capital, but without destroying big capital'.[69] This means that LO has been able to build an organisation which is stable but wedded to its routine. In contrast the LCR has been a much more prominent actor when it comes to anti-fascism and anti-capitalism. But the organisation's diverse membership, much of it forged in movements where the LCR's politics have not been to the fore, shares different views on the role of the party, with some tempted by a radical 'left of the left' coalition with elements of the plural left and others a more revolutionary anti-capitalist formation.

In 1995 Arlette Laguiller, *Lutte Ouvrière*'s presidential candidate, launched a call for a big party of the revolutionary left, only for the organisation to withdraw back to the comfort of small-scale activity. LO therefore failed to capitalise on its electoral success of 1995, when Laguiller won around 1.5 million votes. Prior to this year's poll she revealed that only if LO doubled its 1995 score might the conditions be right to build such a party. Whatever the organisation may declare, however, it is not LO which is setting the conditions, but the urgency of the situation in the factories and streets and offices where its electorate live and work. *Lutte Ouvrière* chose not to take responsibility for its 1995 vote and lived to fight another day. The present situation will be less forgiving. Already some of the dynamic of its recent election success has been lost. Between the two rounds of the election LO took a formally correct position of calling on voters to reject Le Pen but not to give credence to the idea that a republican front could stop him by voting Chirac. At the same time the organisation called on people to demonstrate against the FN. But the present situation demands much more than adopting formally correct positions and waiting for conditions to mature.

Although most of those who demonstrated against Le Pen also voted Chirac, there were a number of problems with this 'republican front'. France, as we have seen, was not about to turn to fascism. The mobilisation of the mainstream right's electorate alone was enough to outnumber Le Pen's vote by two to one. The left, moreover, in advocating electoral unity with the mainstream right has increased the pressure on itself to withdraw in future elections when faced with FN candidates. Le Pen, meanwhile, opposed by an alliance stretching from the employers' association to the Communist Party, was able to present himself as 'the only opposition to the system'.[70] The LCR's decision to effectively call for a vote for Chirac was a concession to this republican front myth, championed so aggressively by the entire establishment between the two rounds of the election. The *Ligue* eventually bowed to this pressure because of its engagement with the movement, in which it played a significant part, reflecting its own difficulties in holding to an independent line within a mass movement. LO, by contrast, did not play a leading role in building the mobilisations. In the absence of such an engagement with the living, active alternative to the republican front, its trenchant rejection of the Chirac vote struck a discordant note with many activists and opened the door to some disgraceful attacks by mainstream politicians insinuating collusion between LO and the far right.

But instead of using the mobilisations as a springboard to launch a united organisation of the revolutionary anti-capitalist left, LO chose instead to attack the LCR for backing a vote for Chirac. The *Ligue*, argued LO, had 'prostituted itself'. Worse still, the organisation then used this as a pretext for rejecting the LCR's call for an electoral agreement in the June 2002 parliamentary elections. In April 2002 the total score of the far left represented twice the number of votes won by LO in 1995. To use Laguiller's own words, this vote underlines the fact that 'something has changed and large numbers of people are aware that workers need an instrument for their defence and that the Communist Party has shown it is no longer that instrument'.[71] Faced with the urgency of the present situation—the decline of social democracy, the resurgence of fascism and the demand from below for a left alternative—LO's rejection of the call for unity is not just sectarian; it represents an outrageous abdication of responsibility. Given the opportunity of engaging with the hundreds of thousands of individuals looking for political solutions to the present crisis and of offering them practical leadership, LO has chosen instead to abstain. A minority within the organisation, no doubt aware that LO is scuppering its chances of playing a political role of any real consequence, has challenged the leadership's stance, and it is to be hoped that others follow. The LCR's response to the election and its aftermath has been incomparably better, calling for forums to be held in the autumn to build a new anti-capitalist left. Meanwhile, those who want to salvage something from the experience of the plural left have moved quickly to attempt to recreate a left reformist current of Greens, Socialists and Communists.[72] There is a battle under way, then, for the future of the left. At stake is the chance to go beyond the existing framework of the left and offer a political home to the many thousands of radicalising voters of 21 April, who are actively seeking one today. Failure to act decisively will allow other forces to regain the initiative. In the coming weeks and months there will inevitably be attempts to revive social democracy with calls for a new 'radical' coalition. Revolutionaries have an unprecedented opportunity to build a viable alternative. This means fighting for a new party which is unflinching and principled in its opposition to fascism, capitalism and war.

Conclusion

Le Pen's presidential score reflects both the FN's organisational durability and the volatility of the context within which it is operating. The organisation's ability to revive after the 1999 split is a product of the deep-seated nature of the crisis of mainstream politics. Le Pen's success, the credibility and prestige which it has brought, will strengthen the organisation in the short term. In the week following the first round results the party claimed to be recruiting between 700 and 1,000 people a day. One striking consequence of Le Pen's success was the willingness of FN voters to express publicly their reasons for voting FN. In contrast, before the first round pollsters had been obliged to double the numbers of people indicating support for the FN because of the sense of shame felt by those making such an admission. The fact that he maintained the support of over 5.5 million people in the second round, in spite of the biggest wave of anti-racist mobilisations ever seen in France, is an indication of how the polarisation of politics in France is intensifying.

There comes a point, then, when pinning the label fascist on Le Pen and denouncing his racism in not enough. Millions of people have shown that they are willing to stomach all this in the hope that Le Pen will bring a strong-arm solution to their problems. Many of these people will only be won away from the FN if they feel another credible alternative is on offer. Countless recent examples show that increasingly combative movements are developing internationally against global capital, neo-liberalism and war: the 3 million strong demonstration in March 2002 against Berlusconi, the biggest in Italy since the war, and the subsequent general strike; the 500,000 who demonstrated against capitalism and war at the European Union summit last spring; and the Argentinian uprising at the turn of the year. In Buenos Aires one of the protesters watched wave upon wave of demonstrators streaming into the city centre. The thought which occured to him—'This is like the fall of the wall. This is the fall of the neo-liberal wall'[72]—expresses a widespread sense that an old order is fading. The polarisation dealt with here is one of the consequences. Those who want to replace that order with something better are increasingly being confronted with situations which require the broadest possible unity in action to deal with an immediate threat—fascism, war, neo-liberal reforms—and the sharpest possible clarity in order that such action is as effective as possible. For those engaged in such struggles, the question of political organisation, how to build unity and offer leadership, is therefore being posed with increasing urgency—and nowhere more so than in France.

Notes

I am grateful to Antoine Boulangé, Sebastian Budgen, Denis Godard, Paul McGarr, Megan Trudell and Helen Wolfreys for their help in the preparation of this article.

1   S Beaud and M Pialoux, 'Emeutes urbaines, violence sociale', *Le Monde Diplomatique*, July 2001.
2   G Filoche, *Le travail jetable non, les 35 heures oui* (Paris, 1999), ch 5.
3   *L'Humanité*, 3 May 2002.
4   *Le Monde*, 28 April 2002.
5   See P Fysh and J Wolfreys, *The Politics of Racism in France* (Macmillan, 1998), ch 3.
6   *The Guardian*, 13 May 2002.
7   *Le Figaro*, 23 April 2002.
8   J Wolfreys, 'Shoes, Lies and Videotape: Corruption and the French State', in *Modern and Contemporary France*, November 2001.
9   G Dufoix, cited in J Wolfreys, 'Protecting Democracy? State Crime by France and its Control', in J I Ross (ed), *Controlling State Crime in Advanced Industrialized Democracies* (New York, 2000).
10 *France 2*, 21 February 2002.
11 P Mauroy, cited in *Le Monde*, 24 April 2002.
12 Yves Mény, 'La Double Mort de la Ve République', *Le Monde*, 23 April 2002.
13 On the period opened up by the 1995 strikes see J Wolfreys, 'Class Struggles in France', *International Socialism* 84 (Autumn 1999).
14 P Poujade, cited in A Rollat, *Les hommes de l'extrême droite* (Paris, 1985) p25.
15 Police report made out by acting chief superintendent of the police district of Algiers, cited ibid, p26.
16 Ibid.

17 See M Abdelbaki in *Libération*, 12 February 1985, and H Kéfamané, *La Pacification*, cited in J Lorien, K Criton and S Dumont, *Le Système Le Pen* (Brussels, 1985), p43.

18 *Le Monde*, 4 May 2002.

19 J-M Le Pen, *Combat*, 9 November 1962.

20 Le Pen, cited in G Pons, *Les Rats Noirs* (Paris, 1977), p150.

21 F Gaucher, *Le Fascisme est-il Actuel?* (Paris, 1961), pp115-116.

22 L Gaultier, cited in *L'Evénement du Jeudi*, 15-21 February 1990.

23 Ibid.

24 Ordre Nouveau, *Pour une Ordre Nouveau* (Paris, 1972), p153.

25 *Ordre Nouveau Hebdo*, 12 October 1972.

26 *Pour une Ordre Nouveau*, op cit, p166.

27 Ibid, p160.

28 Ibid, p100.

29 A Hitler, *Mein Kampf*, cited in F Neumann, *Behemoth* (New York, 1972), p358.

30 *Ordre Nouveau*, Third Congress, 9-11 June 1973. Cited in A Rollat, op cit, pp58-59.

31 *Ordre Nouveau Hebdo*, 18 October 1972.

32 *Cahiers Européens*, May 1974.

33 F Duprat, 'Pour une Théorie Nationaliste', in *Dossier Nationaliste* 1, 1979

34 *Le National*, April 1978.

35 Ibid.

36 Le Pen, interview in *Europe 1*, not dated. Cited in J Lorien et al, op cit, p135.

37 F Duprat, *Cahiers Européens Hebdo: Notre Europe* 18, 18 April 1974.

38 F Duprat, 'Pour une Théorie Nationaliste', op cit.

39 *Le National* 14, September-October 1980.

40 Ibid.

41 See in particular the role of the *'Nouvelle Droite'* in P Fysh and J Wolfreys, op cit, ch 5.

42 P Mauroy, interview with *Nord-Eclair*, cited in *Le Monde*, 29 January 1983.

43 A Bihr, *La Farce Tranquille, Normalisation à la Française* (Paris, 1986), p39.

44 Cited in F Gaspard.*Une Petite Ville en France* (Paris, 1990), p182.

45 J Chirac, cited in E Plenel and A Rollat, *La République Menacée, Dix Ans De l'Effet Le Pen* (Paris, 1992), pp331-333.

46 Cited in E Plenel and A Rollat, op cit, p99.

47 'FN vote (%) = 6 + [1.7 x foreigners] + trace element', H Le Bras, *Les Trois France* (Paris, 1986), p216).

48 C Husbands, 'The Support for the *Front National*: Analyses and Findings', *Ethnic and Racial Studies* (July 1991), p392. Any number of other correlations are also possible. One demonstrator turned up to the May Day protest against Le Pen with a banner showing two maps—one highlighting areas where the FN achieved its highest scores, another with the same areas marked showing contamination from the Chernobyl disaster. 'Is this a coincidence?' read the banner.

49 J Wolfreys, 'Class Struggles in France', op cit.

50 *Libération*, 3 May 1999.

51 P Perrineau, 'Le FN Saisi par la "Debauche Democratique"', *Le Monde des Débats*, March 1999.

52 Document drawn up by Y Blot, *Le Canard Enchaine*, 17 February 1999. Blot later switched back to Le Pen before withdrawing from active politics.

53 *Libération*, 3 May 1999.

54 *Le Monde*, 28 May 1999.

55 *Le Parisien*, 29 April 2000.

56   C Bloch-London and T Coutrot, 'La réduction du temps de travail a-t-elle encore
      un avenir?', in Fondation Copernic, *Un Social Libéralisme à la Française*
      (Paris, 2001).
57   *Libération*, 24 April 2002.
58   L Wacquant, 'Pénalisation de la Misère et Projet Politique Néolibéral', in
      Collectif Contre la Répression, *Répressions, la Cagnotte et le Bâton* (Paris,
      2000). See also L Wacquant, *Les Prisons de la Misère* (Paris, 1999).
59   *Libération*, 24 April 2002.
60   *Le Monde*, 15 September 1999.
61   *Le Monde*, 27 October 1997.
62   *Le Monde*, 28 October 1997.
63   L Trotsky, *Whither France?* (London, 1974), p9.
64   *Financial Times*, 6 May 2002.
65   S Allende, cited in C Marker (dir), *Le Fond de l'Air est Rouge* (1973).
66   Fondation Copernic, *Un Social Libéralisme à la Française*, op cit, p23.
67   *Les Inrockuptibles*, 1-7 May 2002.
68   On this and other questions relating to social movements, see C Barker and G
      Dale, 'Class Will Out? Some Remarks on Social Movements in Europe', paper
      for the European Sociological Association Conference, University of Essex,
      August 1997.
69   L' Économie Capitaliste Mondiale,' *Lutte de Classe*, December 2001.
70   *Le Monde*, 6 May 2002.
71   Arlette Laguiller, Lyon, 18 April 2002.
72   See the appeal for the reconstruction of the left launched by, among others, the
      Communists Patrick Braouezec and Geneviève Fraisse, Marie-Noëlle
      Lienneman of the *Gauche Socialiste*, the Greens Noël Mamère and Dominique
      Voynet (a former minister in the Jospin government) and a host of other
      'personalities' (*Libération*, 29 May 2002).
73   R Carcova, cited in C Harman, 'Argentina: Rebellion at the Sharp End',
      International Socialism 94 (Spring 2002), p4.

Leaps! Leaps! Leaps!

DANIEL BENSAÏD

Hannah Arendt was worried that politics might disappear completely
from the world. The century had seen such disasters that the question of
whether 'politics still has any meaning at all' had become unavoidable.
The issues at stake in these fears were eminently practical: 'The lack of
meaning in which the whole of politics has ended up is confirmed by the
dead end into which specific political questions are flocking'.[1]

For her, the form taken by this feared disappearance of politics was
totalitarianism. Today we are confronted with a different form of the
danger: totalitarianism, the human face of market tyranny. Here politics
finds itself crushed between the order of financial markets—which is
made to seem natural—and the moralising prescriptions of ventriloquist
capitalism. The end of politics and the end of history then coincide in the
infernal repetition of the eternity of the commodity, in which echo the
toneless voices of Fukuyama and Furet: 'The idea of *another* society has
become almost impossible to conceive of, and no one in the world today
is offering any advice on the subject. Here we are, condemned to live in
the world as it is'.[2] This is worse than melancholy—it is despair, as
Blanqui might have said, this eternity of mankind through the Dow Jones
and the FT 100.

Hannah Arendt thought she could set a date on the beginning and end
of politics: inaugurated by Plato and Aristotle, she thought it found 'its
definitive end in the theories of Marx'.[3] Announcing the end of philosophy, Marx is also, by some jest of the dialectic, said to have pronounced

that of politics. This fails to recognise Marx's politics as the only one which is conceivable in the face of capitalised violence and the fetishisms of modernity: 'The state is not valid for everything', he wrote, standing up clearly against 'the presumptuous exaggeration of the political factor' which makes the bureaucratic state into the embodiment of the abstract universal. Rather than a one-sided passion for the social, his effort is directed towards the emergence of a politics of the oppressed starting from the constitution of non-state political bodies which prepare the way for the necessary withering away of the state as a separate body.

The vital, urgent question is that of politics from below, politics for those who are excluded and cut off from the state politics of the ruling class. We have to solve the puzzle of proletarian revolutions and their repeated tragedies: how do we spurn the dust and win the prize? How can a class which is physically and morally stunted in its daily life by the involuntary servitude of forced labour transform itself into the universal subject of human emancipation? Marx's answers on this point derive from a sociological gamble—industrial development leads to the numerical growth and the concentration of the working classes which in turn leads to progress in their organisation and consciousness. The logic of capital itself is thus said to lead to 'the constitution of the proletarians into a ruling class'. Engels' preface to the 1890 edition of the *Communist Manifesto* confirms this assumption: 'For the ultimate triumph of the ideas set forth in the *Manifesto* Marx relied solely and exclusively upon the intellectual development of the working class as it necessarily had to ensue from united action and discussion'.[4] The illusion according to which the winning of universal suffrage would allow the English proletariat, which was a majority in society, to adjust political representation to social reality derives from this gamble. In the same spirit, in his 1898 commentary on the *Manifesto*, Antonio Labriola expressed the view 'that the desired coming together of communists and proletarians is from now on an accomplished fact'. The political emancipation of the proletariat flowed necessarily from its social development.

The convulsive history of the last century shows that we cannot so easily escape from the haunted world of the commodity, from its bloodthirsty gods and from their 'box of repetitions'. Lenin's untimely relevance results necessarily from this observation. If politics today still has a chance of averting the double danger of a naturalisation of the economy and a fatalisation of history, this chance requires a new Leninist act in the conditions of imperial globalisation. Lenin's political thought is that of politics as strategy, of favourable moments and weak links.

The 'homogeneous and empty' time of mechanical progress, without crises or breaks, is a non-political time. The idea maintained by Kautsky of a 'passive accumulation of forces' belongs to this view of time. A primitive version of calm force, this 'socialism outside of time' and at the speed of a tortoise dissolves the uncertainty of the political struggle into the proclaimed laws of historical evolution.

Lenin, on the other hand, thought of politics as a time full of struggle, a time of crises and collapses. For him the specificity of politics is expressed in the concept of a revolutionary crisis, which is not the logical continuation of a 'social movement', but a general crisis of the reciprocal relations between all the classes in society. The crisis is then defined as a 'national crisis'. It acts to lay bare the battle lines, which have been obscured by the mystical phantasmagoria of the commodity. Then alone, and not by virtue of some inevitable historical ripening, can the proletariat be transformed and 'become what it is'.

The revolutionary crisis and political struggle are thus closely linked. 'The knowledge that the working class can have of itself is indissolubly linked to a precise knowledge of the reciprocal relations of all the classes in contemporary society, a knowledge which is not only theoretical, we should rather say which is less theoretical than founded on the experience of politics.' It is indeed through the test of practical politics that this knowledge of the reciprocal relations between classes is acquired. It makes 'our revolution' into a 'revolution of the whole people'.

This approach is the complete opposite of a crude workerism, which reduces the political to the social. Lenin categorically refuses to 'mix the question of classes with that of parties'. The class struggle is not reduced to the antagonism between the worker and his boss. It confronts the proletariat with 'the whole capitalist class' on the level of the process of capitalist production as a whole, which is the object of study in Volume III of *Capital*. This, moreover, is why it is perfectly logical for Marx's unfinished chapter on class to come precisely at this point and not in Volume I on the process of production or Volume II on the process of circulation. As a political party, revolutionary social democracy thus represents the working class, not just in its relations with a group of employers, but also with 'all the classes of contemporary society and with the state as an organised force'.

The time of the propitious moment in Leninist strategy is no longer that of the electoral Penelopes and Danaïdes, whose work is constantly undone again, but that which gives a rhythm to struggle and which is suspended by crisis—the time of the opportune moment and of the singular conjuncture, where necessity and contingency, act and process, history and event are knotted together. 'We should not imagine revolution itself in the form of a singular act: the revolution will be a rapid succession of more or less violent explosions, alternating with phases of more or less deep calm. That is why the essential activity of our party, the essential focus of its activity, must be possible and necessary work both in the periods of the most violent explosion and in those of calm, that is, a work of unified political agitation for all Russia.'

Revolutions have their own tempo, marked by accelerations and slowing down. They also have their own geometry, where the straight line is broken in bifurcation and sudden turns. The party thus appears in a new light. For Lenin, it is no longer the result of a cumulative experience, nor the modest teacher with the task of raising proletarians from the darkness of ignorance to the illumination of reason. It becomes a strategic operator, a sort of gearbox and pointsman of the class struggle. As Walter Benjamin very clearly recognised, the strategic time of politics is not the homogeneous and empty time of classical mechanics, but a broken time, full of knots and wombs pregnant with events.

Without any doubt there is, in the formation of Lenin's thought, an interplay of continuities and breaks. The major breaks (which are not 'epistemological breaks') can be placed in 1902, around *What Is To Be Done?* and *One Step Forward*, or again in 1914-1916, when it was necessary to rethink imperialism and the state amid the twilight of the war and by taking up again the thread of Hegelian logic. At the same time, from *The Development of Capitalism in Russia*, a foundational work, Lenin will establish the framework which will allow him subsequently to make theoretical corrections and strategic adjustments.

The confrontations in the course of which Bolshevism was defined are an expression of this revolution in the revolution. From the polemics of *What Is To Be Done?* and *One Step Forward, Two Steps Back*, the classic texts essentially preserve the idea of a centralised vanguard with military discipline. The real point is elsewhere. Lenin is fighting against the confusion, which he describes as 'disorganising', between the party and the class. The making of a distinction between them has its context in the great controversies then running through the socialist movement, especially in Russia. This is in opposition to the populist, economist and Menshevik currents, which sometimes converge to defend 'pure socialism'. The apparent intransigence of this formal orthodoxy in fact expresses the idea that the democratic revolution must be a necessary stage on the road of historic evolution. While waiting to be strengthened and to achieve the social and electoral majority, the nascent working class movement was supposed to leave the leading role to the bourgeoisie and be satisfied with acting in support of capitalist modernisation. This confidence in the direction of history, where everything would come in due time to those who wait, underlies the orthodox positions of Kautsky in the Second International: we must patiently advance along the 'roads to power' until power falls like a ripe fruit.

For Lenin, on the other hand, it is the goal that orientates the movement; strategy takes precedence over tactics, politics over history. That is why it is necessary to demarcate oneself before uniting, and, in order to unite, 'to utilise every manifestation of discontent, and to gather and turn to the best account every protest, however small'. In other words, to conceive the political struggle as 'far more extensive and complex than the economic struggle of the workers against the employers and the government'.[5] Thus when *Rabocheye Dyelo* deduces the political objectives of economic struggle, Lenin criticises it for 'lowering the level of the many-sided political activity of the proletariat'. It is an illusion to imagine that the 'purely working class movement' is capable by itself of elaborating an independent ideology. The merely spontaneous development of the working class movement on the contrary leads to 'subordinating it to bourgeois ideology'. For the ruling ideology is not a question of the manipulation of consciousness, but the objective result of the fetishism of commodities. Its iron grip and enforced servitude can only be escaped through the revolutionary crisis and the political struggle of parties. This is indeed the Leninist answer to the unsolved puzzle of Marx.

For Lenin everything leads to the conception of politics as the invasion whereby that which was absent becomes present: 'The division into classes is certainly, in the last resort, the most profound basis for political groupings', but this last resort is 'established only by political struggle'. Thus 'communism literally erupts from all points of social life: decidedly it blossoms everywhere. If one of the outlets is blocked with particular care, then the contagion will find another, sometimes the most unexpected.' That is why we cannot know 'which spark will ignite the fire'.

Whence the slogan which, according to Tucholsky, sums up Leninist politics: 'Be ready!' Ready for the improbable, for the unexpected, for what happens. If Lenin could describe politics as 'concentrated economics', this concentration means a qualitative change on the basis of which politics cannot fail to 'have primacy over economics'. 'By advocating the fusion of the economic and political standpoints', Bukharin, on the other hand, 'is sliding towards eclecticism'. Likewise, in his 1921 polemic against the Workers' Opposition, Lenin criticises this 'wretched name' which once again reduces politics to the social and which claims that the management of the national economy should be directly incumbent on the 'producers grouped together in producers' unions', which would come down to reducing the class struggle to a confrontation of sectional interests without synthesis.

Politics, on the contrary, has its own language, grammar and syntax. It has its latencies and its slips. On the political stage, the transfigured class struggle has 'its fullest, most rigorous and best defined expression in the struggle of parties'. Deriving from a specific register, which is not reducible to its immediate determinations, political discourse is more closely related to algebra than to arithmetic. Its necessity is of a different order, 'much more complex', than that of social demands directly linked to the relationship of exploitation. For contrary to what 'vulgar Marxists' imagine, politics 'does not tamely follow economics'. The ideal of the revolutionary militant is not the trade unionist with a narrow horizon, but the 'tribune of the people' who fans the embers of subversion in all spheres of society.

'Leninism', or rather Stalinised 'Leninism' built up as a state orthodoxy, is often made responsible for bureaucratic despotism. The notion of the vanguard party, separate from the class, is thus believed to have contained the germ of the substitution of the apparatus for the real social movement and of all the circles of bureaucratic hell. However unfair it may be, this accusation raises a real difficulty. If politics is not identical with the social, the representation of the one by the other necessarily becomes problematic—on what can its legitimacy be based?

For Lenin, the temptation very much exists of resolving the contradiction by supposing a tendency for representatives to adequately represent their constituents, culminating in the withering away of the political state. The contradictions in representation do not allow for any exclusive agent, and being constantly called into question in the plurality of constitutive forms, they are eliminated at the same time. This aspect of the question risks covering up another, which is no less important, inasmuch as Lenin does not seem to recognise the full extent of his innovation. Thinking that he was paraphrasing a canonical text by Kautsky, he distorted it significantly as follows. Kautsky wrote that 'science' comes to the proletarians 'from outside the class struggle, borne by "the bourgeois intelligentsia".' By an extraordinary verbal shift, Lenin translates this so that 'class political consciousness' (rather than 'science'!) comes 'from outside the economic struggle'[6] (rather than from outside the class struggle, which is political as much as social!), borne no longer by the intellectuals as a social category, but by the party as an agent which specifically structures the political field. The difference is pretty substantial.

Such a constant insistence on the language of politics, where social reality is manifested through a permanent interplay of displacements and condensations, should logically result in a way of thought based on plurality and representation. If the party is not the class, the same class should be represented politically by several parties expressing its differences and contradictions. The representation of the social in the political should then become the object of an institutional and juridical elaboration. Lenin does not go so far. A detailed study, which would go beyond the dimensions of an article like this, of his positions on the national question, on the trade union question in 1921, and on democracy throughout 1917, would enable us to verify it.[7]

Thus he subjects representation to rules inspired by the Paris Commune, aiming to limit political professionalisation: elected representatives to be paid a wage equal to that of a skilled worker, constant vigilance about favours and privileges for office holders, the responsibility of those elected to those who elected them. Contrary to a persistent myth, he did not advocate binding mandates. This was the case in the party: 'the powers of delegates must not be limited by binding mandates'; in the exercise of their powers 'they are completely free and independent'; the congress or assembly is sovereign. Likewise on the level of state organs, where 'the right of recall of deputies' must not be confused with a binding mandate which would reduce representation to the sectional addition of particular interests and narrowly local points of view, without any possible synthesis, which would deprive democratic deliberation of any substance and any relevance.

As for plurality, Lenin constantly affirmed that 'the struggle of shades of opinion' in the party is inevitable and necessary, so long as it takes place within limits 'approved by common agreement'. He maintained 'that it is necessary to include in the party rules guarantees of minority rights, so that the dissatisfactions, irritations and conflicts that will constantly and unavoidably arise may be diverted from the accustomed philistine channels of rows and squabbling into the still unaccustomed channels of a constitutional and dignified struggle for one's convictions. As one of these essential guarantees, we propose that the minority be allowed one or more writers' groups, with the right to be represented at congresses and with complete "freedom of speech".'[8]

If politics is a matter of choice and decision, it implies an organised plurality. This is a question of principles of organisation. As for the system of organisation, this may vary according to concrete circumstances, on condition that it does not lose the guiding thread of principle in the labyrinth of opportunities. Then even the notorious discipline in action seems less sacrosanct than the golden myth of Leninism would have it. We know how Zinoviev and Kamenev were guilty of indiscipline by publicly opposing the insurrection, yet they were not permanently removed from their responsibilities. Lenin himself, in extreme circumstances, did not hesitate to demand a personal right to disobey the party. Thus he considered resigning his responsibilities in order to resume 'freedom to agitate' in the rank and file of the party. At the critical moment of decision, he wrote bluntly to the central committee, 'I have gone where you did not want me to go (to Smolny). Goodbye.'

His own logic led him to envisage plurality and representation in a country with no parliamentary or democratic traditions. But Lenin did not go all the way. There are (at least) two reasons for that. The first is that he had inherited from the French Revolution the illusion that once the oppressor has been removed, the homogenisation of the people (or of the class) is only a matter of time: contradictions among the people can now come only from the other (the foreigner) or from treason. The second is that the distinction between politics and the social is not a guarantee against a fatal inversion: instead of leading to the socialisation of the political, the dictatorship may mean the bureaucratic statification of the social. Did not Lenin himself venture to predict 'the extinction of the struggle between parties in the soviets'?

In *State and Revolution* parties do indeed lose their function in favour of a direct democracy, which is not supposed to be entirely a separate state. But, contrary to initial hopes, the statification of society was victorious over the socialisation of state functions. Absorbed in the main dangers of military encirclement and capitalist restoration, the revolutionaries did not see growing beneath their feet the no less important danger of bureaucratic counter-revolution. Paradoxically, Lenin's weaknesses are linked as much, or even more, to his libertarian inclinations as to his authoritarian temptations, as if a secret link united the two.

The revolutionary crisis appears as the critical moment of the possible resolution, where theory becomes strategy:

> History in general and more particularly the history of revolutions is always richer in its content, more varied, more many-sided, more alive, more ingenious than is conceived by the best parties, the most conscious vanguards of the most advanced classes. And that is understandable since the best vanguards express the consciousness, the will and the passion of tens of thousands of men, while the revolution is one of the moments of special exaltation and tension of all human faculties—the work of the consciousness, the will, the imagination, the passion of hundreds of thousands of men spurred on by the harshest class struggle. Hence two practical conclusions of great importance: first, that the revolutionary class must, in order to carry out its task, be able to take possession of all forms and all aspects of social activity without the slightest exception; secondly, the revolutionary class must be ready to replace one form by another rapidly and without warning.

From this Lenin deduces the need to respond to unexpected events where often the hidden truth of social relations is suddenly revealed:

> We do not and cannot know which spark...will kindle the conflagration, in the sense of raising up the masses; we must, therefore, with our new and commu-

nist principles, set to work to stir up all and sundry, even the oldest, mustiest and seemingly hopeless spheres, for otherwise we shall not be able to cope with our tasks, shall not be comprehensively prepared, shall not be in possession of all the weapons.[9]

Stir up all spheres! Be on the watch for the most unpredictable solutions! Remain ready for the sudden change of forms! Know how to employ all weapons!

These are the maxims of a politics conceived as the art of unexpected events and of the effective possibilities of a determinate conjuncture.

This revolution in politics brings us back to the notion of revolutionary crisis systematised in *The Collapse of the Second International*. It is defined by an interaction between several variable elements in a situation: when those above can no longer govern as they did before; when those below will not tolerate being oppressed as they were before; and when this double impossibility is expressed by a sudden effervescence of the masses. Adopting these criteria Trotsky stresses in his *History of the Russian Revolution* 'that these premises condition each other is obvious. The more decisively and confidently the proletariat acts, the better will it succeed in bringing after it the intermediate layer, the more isolated will be the ruling class, and the more acute its demoralisation. And, on the other hand, a demoralisation of the rulers will pour water into the mill of the revolutionary class'.[10] But the crisis does not guarantee the conditions of its own resolution. That is why Lenin makes the intervention of a revolutionary party into the decisive factor in a critical situation: 'It is not every revolutionary situation that gives rise to a revolution; revolution arises only out of a situation in which the above-mentioned objective changes are accompanied by a subjective change, namely, the ability of the revolutionary *class* to take revolutionary mass action *strong* enough to break (or dislocate) the old government, which never, not even in a period of crisis, "falls", if it is not toppled over'.[11] The crisis can be resolved only by defeat, at the hands of a reaction which will often be murderous, or by the intervention of a resolute subject.

This was very much the interpretation of Leninism in Lukács's *History and Class Consciousness*. Already at the Fifth Congress of the Communist International this earned him the anathema of the Thermidorian Bolshevisers. Lukács in fact insisted on the fact that '*Only the consciousness of the proletariat can point to the way that leads out of the impasse of capitalism.* As long as this consciousness is lacking, the crisis remains permanent, it goes back to its starting-point, repeats the cycle...' Lukács replies that, 'the difference between the period in which the decisive battles are fought and the foregoing period does not lie in the extent and the intensity of the battles themselves. These quantitative changes are merely symptomatic of the fundamental differences in quality which distinguish these struggles from earlier ones... Now, however, the process by which the proletariat becomes independent and "organises itself into a class" is repeated and intensified until the time when the final crisis of capitalism has been reached, the time when the decision comes more and more within the grasp of the proletariat'.[12] This is echoed in the 1930s when Trotsky, facing Nazism and Stalinist reaction, produced a formulation equating the crisis of humanity with the crisis of revolutionary leadership.

Strategy is 'a calculation of mass, speed and time', wrote Chateaubriand. For Sun Tzu, the art of war was already the art of change and of speed. This art required acquiring 'the speed of the hare' and 'coming to a decision immediately', for it is proven that the most famous victory could have turned to defeat 'if battle had been joined a day earlier or a few hours later'. The rule of conduct derived from this is valid for politicians as well as soldiers: 'Never let any opportunity slip, when you find it favourable. The five elements are not everywhere, nor are they equally pure; the four seasons do not follow each other in the same fashion every year; the rising and setting of the sun are not always at the same point on the horizon. Some days are long and others short. The moon waxes and wanes and is not always equally bright. An army that is well led and well disciplined aptly imitates all these variations'.[13]

The notion of revolutionary crisis takes up this lesson of strategy and politicises it. In certain exceptional circumstances the balance of forces reaches a critical point. 'Any disruption of the rhythms produces effects of conflict. It upsets and disturbs. It can also produce a gap in time, to be filled with an invention, with a creation. This happens, individually and socially, only by passing through a crisis.' A gap in time? An exceptional moment? Whereby can arise the unaccomplished fact, which contradicts the fatality of the accomplished fact.

In 1905 Lenin comes together with Sun Tzu in his praise of speed. It is necessary, he says, 'to begin on time', to act 'immediately'. 'Form immediately, in all places, combat groups. We must indeed be able to grasp in flight those "fleeting moments" of which Hegel speaks and which constitute an excellent definition of the dialectic'. For the revolution in Russia is not the organic result of a bourgeois revolution extended into a proletarian revolution, but an 'intertwining' of two revolutions. Whether the probable disaster can be avoided depends on an acute sense of conjuncture. The art of the slogan is an art of the favourable moment. A particular instruction which was valid yesterday may not be so today but may be valid again tomorrow. 'Until 4 July [1917] the slogan of "All power to the soviets" was correct.' After then it was no longer correct. 'At this moment and this moment alone, perhaps for a few days at most, or for a week or two, such a government could survive.'

A few days! A week! On 29 September 1917 Lenin wrote to the hesitating central committee: 'The crisis has matured'.[14] Waiting was becoming a crime. On 1 October he urged them to *'take power at once'*, to *'resort to insurrection at once'*.[15] A few days later he tried again: 'I am writing these lines on 8 October... The success of both the Russian and the world revolution depends on two or three days' fighting'.[16] He still insisted, 'I am writing these lines on the evening of the 24th. The situation is critical in the extreme. In fact it is now absolutely clear that to delay the uprising would be fatal... Everything now hangs by a thread.' So it is necessary to act 'this very evening, this very night'.[17]

'Breaks in gradualness' noted Lenin in the margins of Hegel's *Science of Logic* at the beginning of the war. And he stressed, 'Gradualness explains nothing without leaps. Leaps! Leaps! Leaps!'[18]

Three brief remarks to conclude on the relevance of Lenin today. His strategic thought defines a state of being available to act in relation to whatever event may arise. But this event is not the absolute Event, coming from nowhere, which some people have mentioned with reference to 11 September. It is situated in conditions of historically determined possibility. That is what distinguishes it from the religious miracle. Thus the revolutionary crisis of 1917 and its resolution by insurrection become strategically thinkable in the framework traced by *The Development of Capitalism in Russia*. This dialectical relation between necessity and contingency, structure and break, history and event, lays the basis for the possibility of a politics organised in duration whereas the arbitrarily voluntarist gamble on the sudden explosion of an event may allow us to resist the mood of the times, it generally leads to a stance of aesthetic resistance rather than militant commitment to patiently modify the course of things.

For Lenin—as for Trotsky—the revolutionary crisis is formed and begins in the national arena, which at the time constitutes the framework of the struggle for hegemony, and goes on to take its place in the context of the world revolution. The crisis in which dual power arises is therefore not reduced to an economic crisis or an immediate conflict between wage labour and capital in the process of production. The Leninist question— who will come out on top?—is that of political leadership: which class will be capable of resolving the contradictions which are stifling society, capable of imposing an alternative logic to that of the accumulation of capital, capable of transcending the existing relations of production and opening up a new field of possibilities? The revolutionary crisis is therefore not a simple social crisis but also a national crisis: in Russia as in Germany, in Spain as in China. The question today is doubtless more complex to the extent that capitalist globalisation has reinforced the overlapping of national, continental and world spaces. A revolutionary crisis in a major country would immediately have an international dimension and would require responses in terms that are both national and continental, or even directly global on questions like energy, ecology, armaments policy, movement of migrants etc. It nonetheless remains an illusion to believe that we can evade this difficulty by eliminating the question of the conquest of political power (on the pretext that power today is divorced from territory and scattered everywhere and nowhere) in favour of a rhetoric of 'counter-powers'. Economic, military and cultural powers are perhaps more widely scattered, but they are also more concentrated than ever. You can pretend to ignore power, but it will not ignore you. You can act superior by refusing to take it, but from Catalonia 1937 to Chiapas, via Chile, experience shows right up to this very day that it will not hesitate to take you in the most brutal fashion. In a word, a strategy of counter-power only has any meaning in the perspective of dual power and its resolution. Who will come out on top?

Finally, detractors often identify 'Leninism' and Lenin himself with a historical form of the political party which is said to have died along with the collapse of the bureaucratic party-states. In this hasty judgement there is a lot of historical ignorance and political frivolity, which can be only partially explained by the traumatism of Stalinist practices. The experience of the past century poses the question of bureaucratisation as a social phenomenon, rather than the question of the form of vanguard party inherited from *What Is To Be Done?* For mass organisations (not only political ones, but equally trade unions and associations) are far from being the least bureaucratic: in France the cases of the CFDT, of the Socialist Party, of the allegedly renovated Communist Party, or of the Greens, are absolutely eloquent on this point. But on the other hand—as we have mentioned—in the Leninist distinction of party and class there are some fertile trails for thinking about the relations between social movements and political representation. Likewise in the superficially disparaged principles of democratic centralism, detractors stress primarily the bureaucratic hypercentralism exemplified in sinister fashion by the Stalinist parties. But a certain degree of centralisation, far from being opposed to democracy, is the essential condition for it to exist— because the delimitation of the party is a means of resisting the decomposing effects of the dominant ideology, and also of aiming at a certain equality between members, counter to the inequalities which are inevitably generated by social relations and by the division of labour. Today we can see very well how the weakening of these principles, far from favouring a higher form of democracy, leads to co-option by the media and the legitimisation by a plebiscite of leaders who are even less controlled by the rank and file. Moreover, the democracy in a revolutionary party aims to produce decisions which are assumed collectively in order to act on the balance of forces. When the superficial detractors of Leninism claim to have freed themselves from a stifling discipline, they are in fact emptying discussion of all its relevance, reducing it to a forum of opinions which does not commit anybody: after an exchange of free speech without any common decision, everyone can leave as they came and no shared practice makes it possible to test the validity of the opposing positions under consideration. Finally, the stress laid—in particular by recycled bureaucrats from the former Communist parties—on the crisis of the party form often enables them to avoid talking about the crisis of the programmatic content and justifies the absence of strategic preoccupation.

A politics without parties (whatever name—movement, organisation, league, party—that they are given) ends up in most cases as a politics without politics: either an aimless tailism towards the spontaneity of social movements, or the worst form of elitist individualist vanguardism, or finally a repression of the political in favour of the aesthetic or the ethical.

Notes

1   H Arendt, *Was ist Politik?* (Munich, 1993), pp28, 31.
2   F Furet, *The Passing of an Illusion* (Chicago, 1999), p502.
3   H Arendt, op cit, p146.
4   K Marx and F Engels, *Collected Works,* vol 27 (London, 1975ff), p59.
5   V I Lenin, *Collected Works,* vol 5 (Moscow, 1960), pp430, 452.
6   Ibid, pp383, 422.
7   Thus in the 1915 debate on ultra-imperialism, Lenin perceives the danger of a new economism whereby the maturity of the capitalist relations of production on the world scale would be a prelude to a final collapse of the system. We again find this concern to avoid any reduction of the political to the economic or the social in the debates of the early 1920s on the characterisation of the Soviet state. To those who speak of a workers' state, Lenin replies that 'the whole point is that it is not quite a workers' state'. His formulation is then more descriptive and complex than a sociological characterisation: it is a workers' and peasants' state *'with a bureaucratic twist to it'*, and 'there you have the reality of the transition' [V I Lenin, op cit, vol 32, p24]. Finally, in the debate on the trade unions, Lenin again defends an original position: because they are not an organ of political power, the unions must not be transformed into 'coercive state organisations'.
8   V I Lenin, op cit, vol 7, p450.
9   V I Lenin, op cit, vol 31, p99.
10   L Trotsky, *The History of the Russian Revolution* (London, 1997), p1024.
11   V I Lenin, op cit, vol 21, p214.
12   G Lukács, *History and Class Consciousness* (London, 1971), pp76, 313.
13   H Lefebvre, *Eléments de rythmanalyse* (Paris, 1996).
14   V I Lenin, op cit, vol 26, p82.
15   Ibid, p140-141.
16   Ibid, pp 179-181.
17   Ibid, p234.
18   V I Lenin, op cit, vol 38, p123.

A cyberspace Lenin: why not?

SLAVOJ ŽIŽEK

If there is a consensus among (whatever remains of) today's radical left, it is that, in order to resuscitate the radical political project, one should leave behind the Leninist legacy: the ruthless focusing on the class struggle, the party as the privileged form of organisation, the violent revolutionary seizure of power, the ensuing 'dictatorship of the proletariat'…are all these not 'zombie-concepts' to be abandoned if the left is to have any chance in the conditions of 'post-industrial' late capitalism?

The problem with this apparently convincing argument is that it endorses all too easily the inherited image of Lenin the wise revolutionary leader who, after formulating the basic co-ordinates of his thought and practice in *What Is to Be Done?*, just consistently and ruthlessly pursued them. What if there is another story about Lenin to be told? It is true that today's left is undergoing a shattering experience of the end of an entire epoch of the progressive movement, the experience of which compels it to reinvent the very basic co-ordinates of its project—however, an exactly homologous experience was what gave birth to Leninism. Recall Lenin's shock when, in the autumn of 1914, all European Social Democratic parties (with the honourable exception of the Russian Bolsheviks and the Serb Social Democrats) adopted the 'patriotic line'—Lenin even thought that the issue of *Vorwärts*, the daily newspaper of German Social Democracy, which reported how Social Democrats in the Reichstag had voted for the war credits, was a forgery of the Russian secret police designed to deceive the Russian workers. In that era of military conflict that cut the European continent in half, how difficult it was to reject the notion that one should take sides in this conflict, and to fight against the 'patriotic fervour' in one's own country! How many great minds (including Freud) succumbed to the nationalist temptation, even if only for a couple of weeks! This shock of 1914 was—to put it in Alain Badiou's terms—a *désastre*, a catastrophe in which an entire world disappeared: not only the idyllic bourgeois faith in progress, but *also* the socialist movement which accompanied it. Lenin himself (the Lenin of *What Is to Be Done?*) lost the ground under his feet—there is, in his desperate reaction, no satisfaction, no 'I told you so!' This moment of *Verzweiflung*, *this* catastrophe, opened up the site for the Leninist event, for breaking the evolutionary historicism of the Second International—and only Lenin was at the level of this opening, the one to articulate the truth of the catastrophe. *This* is the Lenin from which we still have something to learn. The greatness of Lenin was that, in this catastrophic situation, he wasn't afraid to succeed—in contrast to the negative pathos discernible from Rosa Luxemburg to Adorno, for whom the ultimate authentic act is the admission of failure which brings the truth to light. In 1917, instead of waiting for the right moment of maturity, Lenin organised a pre-emptive strike. In 1920, as the leader of the party of the working class with no working class (most of it having been killed in the civil war), he went on organising a state, fully accepting the paradox of the party which has to organise, recreate even, its own base, its working class.

Nowhere is this greatness more palpable than in Lenin's writings which cover the time span from February 1917, when the first revolution abolished Tsarism and installed a democratic regime, to the second revolution in October. In February, Lenin was a half-anonymous political emigré, stranded in Zurich, with no reliable contacts in Russia, mostly learning about events from the Swiss press. In October he led the first successful socialist revolution—so what happened in between? In February, Lenin immediately perceived the revolutionary chance, the result of unique contingent circumstances—if the moment was not seized, the chance for the revolution would be forfeited, perhaps for decades. In his stubborn insistence that one should take the risk and pass to the next stage, ie *repeat* the revolution, Lenin was alone, ridiculed by the majority of the central committee members of his own party, and the reading of Lenin's texts from 1917 provides a unique glimpse into the obstinate, patient and often frustrating, revolutionary work through which Lenin imposed his vision. However, indispensable as Lenin's personal intervention was, one should not modify the story of the October Revolution into that of the lone genius confronted with the disoriented masses and gradually imposing his vision. Lenin succeeded because his appeal, while bypassing the party *nomenklatura*, found an echo in what one is tempted to call revolutionary micropolitics: the incredible explosion of grassroots democracy, of local committees sprouting up all around Russia's big cities and, while ignoring the authority of the 'legitimate' government, taking things into their hands. This is the untold story of the October Revolution.

The first thing to strike the eye of today's reader is how directly readable Lenin's texts from 1917 are. There is no need for long explanatory notes—even if the strange-sounding names are unknown to us, we immediately get what was at stake. From today's distance the texts display an almost classical clarity of the contours of the struggle in which they participate. Lenin is fully aware of the paradox of the situation: in the spring of 1917, after the February Revolution which toppled the Tsarist regime, Russia was the most democratic country in the whole of Europe, with an unprecedented degree of mass mobilisation, freedom of organisation and freedom of the press—and yet this freedom rendered the situation non-transparent, thoroughly ambiguous. If there is a common thread that runs through all Lenin's texts written 'in between the two revolutions' (the February one and the October one), it is his insistence on the gap which separates the 'explicit' formal contours of the political struggle between the multitude of parties and other political subjects from its actual social stakes (immediate peace, the distribution of land, and, of course, 'all power to the soviets', ie the dismantling of the existing state apparatus and its replacement with the new commune-like forms of social management).

This gap—the repetition of the gap between 1789 and 1793 in the French Revolution—is the very space of Lenin's unique intervention: the fundamental lesson of revolutionary materialism is that revolution must strike twice, and for essential reasons. The gap is not simply the gap between form and content. What the 'first revolution' misses is not the content, but the form itself—it remains stuck in the old form, thinking that freedom and justice can be accomplished if we simply put to use the already existing state apparatus and its democratic mechanisms. What if the 'good' party wins the free elections and 'legally' implements socialist transformation? (The clearest expression of this illusion, bordering on the ridiculous, is Karl Kautsky's thesis, formulated in the 1920s, that the logical political form of the first stage of socialism, of the passage from capitalism to socialism, is the parliamentary coalition of bourgeois and proletarian parties.) The parallel here is perfect with the era of early modernity, in which the opposition to the church's ideological hegemony first articulated itself in the very form of another religious ideology, as a heresy. Along the same lines, the partisans of the 'first revolution' want to subvert the capitalist domination within the very political form of capitalist democracy. This is the Hegelian 'negation of the negation': first the old order is negated within its own ideologico-political form; then this form itself has to be negated. Those who oscillate, those who are afraid to make the second step of overcoming this form itself, are those who (to repeat Robespierre) want a 'revolution without revolution'—and Lenin displays all the strength of his 'hermeneutics of suspicion' in discerning the different forms of this retreat.

In his writings of 1917 Lenin saves his utmost acerbic irony for those who engage in the endless search for some kind of 'guarantee' for the revolution. This guarantee assumes two main forms: either the reified notion of social necessity (one should not risk the revolution too early; one has to wait for the right moment, when the situation is 'mature' with regard to the laws of historical development: 'it is too early for the socialist revolution—the working class is not yet mature') or the norma-tive ('democratic') legitimacy ('the majority of the population is not on our side, so the revolution would not really be democratic')—as Lenin repeatedly puts, as if, before the revolutionary agent risks the seizure of state power, it should get permission from some figure of the big Other (organise a referendum which will ascertain that the majority supports the revolution). With Lenin, as with Lacan, the point is that the revolution can only be authorised by itself: one should assume the revo-lutionary *act* is not covered by the big Other—the fear of taking power 'prematurely', the search for a guarantee, is the fear of the abyss of the act. Therein resides the ultimate dimension of what Lenin incessantly denounces as 'opportunism', and his wager is that 'opportunism' is a position which is in itself inherently false, masking fear to accomplish the act with the protective screen of 'objective' facts, laws or norms.

Lenin's answer is not the reference to a *different* set of 'objective facts', but the repetition of the argument made a decade before by Rosa Luxemburg against Kautsky: those who wait for the objective conditions of the revolution to arrive will wait forever—such a position of the objec-tive observer (and not of an engaged agent) is itself the main obstacle to the revolution. Lenin's counter-argument against the formal-democratic critics of the second step is that this 'pure democratic' option itself is utopian: in the concrete Russian circumstances, the bourgeois-democratic state has no chances of surviving—the only 'realistic' way to protect the true gains of the February Revolution (freedom of organisation and the press, etc) is to move forward to the socialist revolution—otherwise the Tsarist reaction will win.

We have here two models, two incompatible logics, of the revolution: those who wait for the ripe teleological moment of the final crisis when revolution will explode 'at its own proper time' by the necessity of historical evolution; and those who are aware that revolution has no 'proper time', those who perceive the revolutionary chance as something that emerges and has to be seized in the very detours of 'normal' historical development. Lenin is not a voluntarist 'subjectivist'—what he insists on is that the exception (the extraordinary set of circumstances, like those in Russia in 1917) offers a way to undermine the norm itself. And is this line of argument, this fundamental stance, not more actual today than ever? Do we not also live in an era when the state and its apparatus, inclusive of its political agents, are simply less and less able to articulate the key issues (ecology, degrading healthcare, poverty, the role of multinational companies, etc)? The only logical conclusion is that a new form of politicisation is urgent, which will directly 'socialise' these crucial issues. The illusion of 1917 that the pressing problems which faced Russia (peace, land distribution, etc) could have been solved through 'legal' parliamentary means is the same as today's illusion that, say, the ecological threat could be avoided by way of expanding the market logic to ecology (making the polluters pay the price for the damage they cause). However, how relevant are Lenin's specific insights here? According to orthodox thinking, Lenin's declining faith in the creative capacities of the masses in the years after the October Revolution led him to emphasise the role of science and the scientists, to rely on the authority of the expert. He hailed 'the beginning of that very happy time when politics will recede into the background...and engineers and agronomists will do most of the talking'.[1] Technocratic post-politics? Lenin's ideas about how the road to socialism runs through the terrain of monopoly capitalism may appear dangerously naive today:

> *Capitalism has created an accounting apparatus in the shape of the banks, syndicates, postal service, consumers' societies, and office employees' unions. Without big banks socialism would be impossible...our task is here merely to lop off what capitalistically mutilates this excellent apparatus, to make it even bigger, even more democratic, even more comprehensive... This will be country-wide book-keeping, country-wide accounting of the production and distribution of goods; this will be, so to speak, something in the nature of the skeleton of socialist society.[2]*

Is this not the most radical expression of Marx's notion of the general intellect regulating all social life in a transparent way, of the post-political world in which 'administration of people' is supplanted by 'administration of things'? It is, of course, easy to play against this quote the tune of the 'critique of instrumental reason' and 'administered world [*verwaltete Welt*]'. The 'totalitarian' potential is inscribed in this very form of total social control. It is easy to remark sarcastically how, in the Stalinist epoch, the apparatus of social administration effectively became 'even bigger'. Furthermore, is this post-political vision not the very opposite of the Maoist notion of the eternity of the class struggle ('everything is political')?

Are things really so unambiguous, however? What if one replaces the (obviously dated) example of the central bank with the world wide web, today's perfect candidate for the General Intellect? Dorothy Sayers claimed that Aristotle's *Poetics* is effectively the theory of detective novels before they were written—since the poor Aristotle didn't yet know of the detective novel, he had to refer to the only examples at his disposal, the tragedies... Along the same lines, Lenin was effectively developing the theory of the role of the world wide web, but, since the web was unknown to him, he had to refer to the unfortunate central banks. Consequently, can one also say that 'without the world wide web socialism would be impossible...our task here is merely to lop off what capitalistically mutilates this excellent apparatus, to make it even bigger, even more democratic, even more comprehensive'? In these conditions, one is tempted to resuscitate the old, opprobrious and half forgotten Marxian dialectics of the productive forces and the relations of production. It is already commonplace to claim that, ironically, it was these very dialectics which buried 'really existing socialism': socialism was not able to sustain the passage from industrial to post-industrial economy. One of the tragi-comic victims of the disintegration of socialism in ex-Yugoslavia was an old Communist apparatchik interviewed by Ljubljana student radio in 1988. Communists knew they were losing power, so they desperately tried to please everyone. When this old cadre was asked provocative questions about his sex life by the student reporters, he also desperately tried to prove that he was in touch with the young generation. Since, however, the only language he knew was wooden bureaucratese, the result was an uncanny obscene mixture—statements like, 'Sexuality is an important component of my daily activity. Touching my wife between her thighs gives me great new incentives for my work of building socialism.' And when one reads East German official documents from the 1970s and early 1980s, formulating their project of turning the GDR into a kind of Silicon Valley of the Eastern European Socialist bloc, one cannot avoid the impression of the same tragi-comic gap between form and content. While they were fully aware that digitalisation was the way of the future, they approached it in the terms of the old socialist logic of industrial central planning—their very words betrayed the fact that they were not getting what is effectively going on, the social consequences of digitalisation. However, does capitalism really provide the 'natural' frame of the relations of production for the digital universe? Is there not also an explosive potential for capitalism itself in the world wide web? Is not the lesson of the Microsoft monopoly precisely the Leninist one: instead of fighting its monopoly through the state apparatus (recall the court-ordered split of the Microsoft corporation), would it not be more 'logical' just to *socialise* it, rendering it freely accessible? Today one is thus tempted to paraphrase Lenin's well-known motto, 'Socialism = electrification + the power of the soviets': 'Socialism = free access to internet + the power of the soviets.'

In this context, the myth to be debunked is that of the diminishing role of the state. What we are witnessing today is the shift in its functions: while partially withdrawing from its welfare functions, the state is strengthening its apparatus in other domains of social regulation. In order to start a business now one has to rely on the state to guarantee not only law and order, but the entire infrastructure (access to water and energy, means of transportation, ecological criteria, international regulations, etc), to an incomparably larger extent than 100 years ago. Last year's electricity supply debacle in California makes this point palpable: for a couple of weeks in January and February 2001 the privatisation ('deregulation') of the electricity supply changed Southern California, one of the most highly developed 'post-industrial' landscapes in the entire world, into a Third World country with regular blackouts. Of course, the defenders of deregulation claimed that it was not thorough enough, thereby engaging in the old false syllogism of, 'My fiancée is never late for the appointment, because the moment she is late, she is no longer my fiancée': deregulation by definition works, so if it doesn't work, it wasn't truly deregulation... Does the recent mad cow disease panic (which probably presages dozens of similar phenomena which await us in the near future) also not point towards the need for a strict state and global institutionalised control of agriculture?

So what about the basic reproach according to which Lenin is irrelevant for us today because he remained stuck within the horizon of industrial mass production (recall his celebration of Fordism)? How does the passage from factory production to 'post-industrial' production change these co-ordinates? How are we to situate not only the Third World manual labour sweatshops, but the *digital* sweatshops, like the one in Bangalore in which tens of thousands of Indians are programming software for Western corporations? Is it adequate to designate these Indians as the 'intellectual proletariat'? Will they be the final revenge of the Third World? What are the consequences of the (for the conservative Germans, at least) unsettling fact that, after decades of importing hundreds of thousands of manual immigrant workers, Germany has now discovered that it needs at least tens of thousands of intellectual immigrant workers, mostly computer programmers? The disabling alternative of today's Marxism is, what to do apropos of this growing importance of 'immaterial production' today (cyber-workers)? Do we insist that only those involved in 'real' material production are the working class, or do we accomplish the fateful step of accepting that the 'symbolic workers' are the (true) proletarians today? One should resist this step, because it obfuscates the *division* between immaterial and material production, the *split* in the working class between (as a rule geographically separated) cyber-workers and material workers (programmers in the US or India, the sweatshops in China or Indonesia).

Perhaps it is the figure of the *unemployed* who stands for the pure proletarian today: the unemployed's substantial determination remains that of a worker, but they are prevented from actualising it *or* from renouncing it, so they remain suspended in the potentiality of workers who cannot work. Perhaps we are today in a sense 'all jobless'—jobs tend to be more and more based on short term contracts, so that the jobless state is the rule, the zero level, and the temporary job the exception. This, then, should also be the answer to the advocates of 'post-industrial society' whose message to workers is that their time is over, that their very existence is obsolete, and that all they can count on is purely humanitarian compassion—there is less and less place for workers in the universe of today's *capital*, and one should draw the only consistent conclusion from this fact. If today's 'post-industrial' society needs fewer and fewer workers to reproduce itself (20 percent of the workforce, on some accounts), then it is not workers who are in excess, but capital itself.

The key antagonism of the so called new (digital) industries is thus: how to maintain the form of (private) property, within which only the logic of profit can be maintained (see also the Napster problem, the free circulation of music)? And do the legal complications in biogenetics not point in the same direction? The key element of the new international trade agreements is the 'protection of intellectual property'—whenever, in a merger, a big Western company takes over a Third World company, the first thing they do is close down the research department. Phenomena emerge here which involve the notion of property in extraordinary dialectical paradoxes: in India, local communities suddenly discover that medical practices and materials they have been using for centuries are now owned by American companies, so they should be bought from them; with the biogenetic companies patenting genes, we are all discovering that parts of ourselves, our genetic components, are already copyrighted, owned by others.

However, the outcome of this crisis of private property of the means of production is by no means guaranteed—it is *here* that one should take into account the ultimate paradox of Stalinist society. Against the capitalism which is the class society, but in principle egalitarian, without direct hierarchical divisions, 'mature' Stalinism is a classless society articulated in precisely defined hierarchical groups (top *nomenklatura*, technical workers, army, etc). What this means is that, already for Stalinism, the classic Marxist notion of the class struggle is no longer adequate to describe its hierarchy and domination—in the Soviet Union from the late 1920s onwards the key social division was not defined by property, but by direct access to power mechanisms and to privileged material and cultural conditions of life (food, accommodation, health-care, freedom of travel, education). And perhaps the ultimate irony of history will be that, in the same way, Lenin's vision of 'central bank socialism' can be properly read only retroactively, from today's world wide web. The Soviet Union provided the first model of the developed 'post-property' society, of the true 'late capitalism' in which the ruling class will be defined by direct access to the (informational, administra-tive) means of social power and control and to other material and social privileges: the point will no longer be to own companies, but directly to run them, to have the right to use a private jet, to have access to top healthcare, etc—privileges which will be acquired not by property, but by other mechanisms (educational, managerial, etc).

This, then, is the forthcoming crisis which will offer the perspective of a new emancipatory struggle, of the thorough reinvention of the political—not the old Marxist choice between private property and its socialisation, but the choice between the hierarchical and egalitarian post-property society. Here the old Marxist thesis on how bourgeois freedom and equality are based on private property and market condi-tions acquires an unexpected twist: what market relations enable are (at least) 'formal' freedom and 'legal' equality—since social hierarchy can be sustained through property, there is no need for its direct political assertion. If, then, the role of private property is diminishing, the danger is that this gradual vanishing will create the need for some new (racist or expert-rule) form of hierarchy, directly founded on individuals' properties, and thus cancelling even 'formal' bourgeois equality and freedom. In short, in so far as the determining factor of social power will be the inclusion/exclusion from the privileged set (of access to knowledge, control, etc), we can expect the rise of the different modes of exclusion, up to direct racism. The first clear sign which points in this direction is the new alliance between politics (government) and natural sciences. In the newly emerging biopolitics, the government is insti-gating 'embryo industry', the control over our genetic legacy outside democratic control, justified by an offer no one can refuse: 'Don't you want to be cured of cancer, diabetes, Alzheimer's…?' However, while politicians are making such 'scientific' promises, scientists themselves remain deeply sceptical, often emphasising the need for decisions reached through a large social consensus.

The ultimate problem of genetic engineering does not reside in its unpredictable consequences (what if we create monsters—say, humans with no sense of moral responsibility?), but in the way biogenetic engineering fundamentally affects our notion of education: instead of educating a child to be a good musician, will it be possible to manipulate his genes so that he will be 'spontaneously' inclined towards music? Instead of instilling in him a sense of discipline, will it be possible to manipulate his genes so that he will 'spontaneously' tend to obey orders? The situation is here radically open—if two classes of people will gradually emerge, the 'naturally born' ones and the genetically manipulated ones, it is not even clear in advance which class will occupy the higher level in social hierarchy. Will the 'naturals' consider the manipulated ones as mere tools, not truly free beings, or will the much more perfect manipulated ones consider 'naturals' as belonging to a lower level of evolution?

The forthcoming struggle thus has no guaranteed outcome—it will confront us with an unheard-of urgency to act, since it will concern not only a new mode of production, but a radical rupture in what it means to be a human being. Today we can already discern the signs of a kind of general unease—recall the series of events usually listed under the name of 'Seattle'. The ten-year honeymoon of triumphant global capitalism is over, the long overdue 'seven year itch' is here—witness the panicky reactions of the big media, which, from *Time* magazine to CNN, all of a sudden started to warn about Marxists manipulating the crowd of 'honest' protesters. The problem is now the strictly Leninist one—how to *actualise* the media's accusations, how to invent the organisational structure which will confer on this unrest the *form* of the universal political demand. Otherwise the momentum will be lost, and what will remain is marginal disturbance, perhaps organised as a new Greenpeace, with a certain efficiency, but also strictly limited goals, marketing strategy, etc. In other words, the key 'Leninist' lesson today is that politics without the organisational *form* of the party is politics without politics, so the answer to those who want just the (quite adequately named) 'new *social* movements' is the same as the answer of the Jacobins to the Girondin compromisers: 'You want revolution without a revolution!' Today's obstacle is that there seem to be only two ways open for socio-political engagement: either play the game of the system, engage in the 'long march through the institutions', or get active in new social movements, from feminism through ecology to anti-racism. And again the limit of these movements is that they are not *political* in the sense of the Universal Singular; they are 'single-issue movements' which lack the dimension of universality, ie they do not relate to the social *totality*.

The promise of the 'Seattle' movement resides in the fact that it is the very opposite of its usual media designation (the 'anti-globalisation protest'); it is the first kernel of a new *global* movement, global with regard to its content (it aims at a global confrontation with today's capitalism) as well as to its form (it is a global movement, involving a mobile international network, able to react from Seattle to Prague). It is *more* global than 'global capitalism', since it brings into the game its victims, ie those *excluded* by capitalist globalisation. Perhaps one should take the risk and apply Hegel's old distinction between 'abstract' and 'concrete' universality here: the capitalist globalisation is 'abstract', focused on the speculative movement of capital, while the 'Seattle' movement stands for 'concrete universality', ie for the totality of global capitalism *and* its excluded dark side.

Here Lenin's reproach to liberals is crucial: they only *exploit* the working classes' discontent to strengthen their position vis-à-vis the conservatives, instead of identifying with it to the end.[3] Is this not also the case with today's left liberals? They like to evoke racism, ecology, workers' grievances, etc, to score points over the conservatives *without endangering the system*. Recall how, in Seattle, Bill Clinton himself deftly referred to the protesters on the streets outside, reminding the gathered leaders inside the guarded palaces that they should listen to the message of the demonstrators (the message which, of course, Clinton interpreted, depriving it of its subversive sting attributed to the dangerous extremists introducing chaos and violence into the majority of peaceful protesters). This Clintonesque stance later developed into an elaborated 'carrot and stick' strategy of containment: on the one hand, paranoia (the notion that there is a dark Marxist plot lurking behind); on the other hand, in Genoa, none other than Berlusconi provided food and shelter to the anti-globalisation demonstrators—on condition that they 'behaved properly' and *didn't disturb* the official event. It's the same with all new social movements, up to the Zapatistas in Chiapas. Systemic politics is always ready to 'listen to their demands', depriving them of their proper political sting. The true 'third way' we have to look for is this third way between institutionalised parliamentary politics and the new social movements.

As a sign of this emerging uneasiness and need for a true third way, it is interesting to see how, in a recent interview, even a conservative liberal like John le Carré had to admit that, as a consequence of the 'love affair between Thatcher and Reagan', in most of the developed Western countries and especially in the United Kingdom 'the social infrastructure has practically stopped working', which then leads him to make a direct plea

for, at least, 'renationalising the railways and water'.[4] We are effectively
approaching a state in which (selective) private affluence is accompanied
by the global (ecological, infrastructural) degradation which will soon
start to affect us all: the quality of water is a problem not only in the
UK—a recent survey showed that the entire basin out of which the Los
Angeles area draws its water is already so affected by man-made toxic
chemicals that it will soon be impossible to render it drinkable, even
through the use of the most advanced filters. Le Carré formulated his fury
at Blair for accepting the Thatcherite basic co-ordinates in very precise
terms: 'I thought last time, in 1997, that he was lying when he denied he
was a socialist. The worst thing I can say about him is that he was telling
the truth'.[5] More precisely, even if, in 1997, Blair was 'subjectively'
lying, even if his secret agenda was to save whatever is possible of the
socialist agenda, he was 'objectively' telling the truth: his (eventual) subjective socialist conviction was a self deception, an illusion which
enabled him to fulfil his 'objective' role, that of finishing the Thatcherite
'revolution'.

The ultimate answer to the reproach that the radical left's proposals
are utopian should thus be that today the true utopia is the belief that the
present liberal-democratic capitalist consensus could go on indefinitely,
without radical changes. We are thus back at the old 1968 motto '*Soyons
réalistes, demandons l'impossible!*' ('Be realistic—demand the impossible!'): in order to be truly a 'realist', one must consider breaking out of
the constraints of what appears 'possible' (or, as we usually term it, 'feasible'). If there is a lesson to be learned from Silvio Berlusconi's
electoral victory in May 2001, it is that the true utopians are the Third
Way leftists—why? The main temptation to be avoided apropos
Berlusconi's victory in Italy is to use it as a pretext for yet another exercise in the tradition of the conservative-leftist *Kulturkritik* (from Adorno
to Virilio), which bemoans the stupidity of the manipulated masses, and
the eclipse of the autonomous individual capable of critical reflection.
This, however, does not mean that the consequences of this victory are to
be underestimated. Hegel said that all historical events have to happen
twice: Napoleon had to lose twice, etc. And it seems that Berlusconi also
had to win the election twice for us to become aware of the full consequences of this event.

So what did Berlusconi achieve? His victory provides a sad lesson
about the role of morality in politics: the ultimate outcome of the great
moral-political catharsis—the anti-corruption campaign of 'clean hands'
which, a decade ago, ruined Christian Democracy and with it the ideological polarity of Christian Democrats and Communists which
dominated post-war Italian politics—is Berlusconi in power. It is something like Rupert Murdoch winning the British elections—a political

movement run as a business-publicity enterprise. Berlusconi's Forza Italia is no longer a political party, but—as its name indicates—rather a sports fan club. If, in the good old Socialist countries, sport was directly politicised (recall the enormous investments that the GDR put into its top athletes), now politics itself is turned into a sports contest. And the parallel goes even further: if the Communist regimes were nationalising the industry, Berlusconi is in a way privatising the state itself. For this reason, all the worry of the leftists and liberal democrats about the danger of neo-fascism lurking beneath Berlusconi's victory is misplaced and in a way much too optimistic: fascism is still a determinate political project, while, in the case of Berlusconi, there is ultimately *nothing* lurking beneath, no secret ideological project, just the sheer assurance that things will function, that we shall do it better. In short, Berlusconi is post-politics at its *purest*. The ultimate sign of 'post-politics' in all Western countries is the growth of a managerial approach to government. Government is reconceived as a managerial function, deprived of its properly political dimension.

The true stake of today's political struggles is, which of the old two main parties, conservatives or the 'moderate left', will succeed in presenting itself as truly embodying the post-ideological spirit, against the other party dismissed as 'still caught in the old ideological spectres'? If the 1980s belonged to the conservatives, the lesson of the 1990s seemed to be that, in our late capitalist societies, Third Way social democracy (or, even more pointedly, post-Communists in the ex-Socialist countries) effectively functions as the representative of capital *as such*, in general, against its particular factions represented by the different 'conservative' parties which, in order to present themselves as addressing the entire population, also try to satisfy the particular demands of the anti-capitalist strata (say, of the domestic 'patriotic' middle class workers threatened by the cheap labour of immigrants. Recall the CDU, which, against the Social Democratic proposal that Germany should import 50,000 Indian computer programmers, launched the infamous motto *'Kinder statt Inder!'*—'Children instead of Indians!') This economic constellation explains to a good degree how and why the Third Way social democrats can simultaneously stand for the interests of big capital and for multiculturalist tolerance which aims at protecting the interests of the foreign minorities.

The Third Way dream of the left was that the pact with the devil may work out: okay, no revolution, we accept capitalism as the only game in town, but at least we will be able to save some of the achievements of the welfare state, plus build a society tolerant towards sexual, religious, and ethnic minorities. If the trend announced by Berlusconi's victory persists, a much darker prospect is discernible on the horizon: a world in which the unlimited rule of capital is not supplemented by left-liberal tolerance, but by the typical post-political mixture of pure publicity-seeking spectacle and Moral Majority concerns (remember that the Vatican gave its tacit support to Berlusconi). If there is a hidden ideological agenda of Berlusconi's 'post-politics', it is, to put it bluntly, the disintegration of the fundamental post Second World War democratic pact. In recent years, there were already numerous signs of the post Second World War anti-fascist pact slowly cracking—from 'revisionist' historians to the New Right populists, so called 'taboos' are falling down. Paradoxically, those who undermine this pact refer to the very liberal universalised logic of victimisation: sure, there were victims of fascism, but what about other victims of the post Second World War expulsions? What about the Germans evicted from their homes in Czechoslovakia? Do they not also have some right to (financial) compensation?

The immediate future does not belong to outright rightist provocateurs like Le Pen or Pat Buchanan, but to people like Berlusconi and Haider, these advocates of global capital in the wolves' clothes of populist nation-alism. The struggle between them and the Third Way left is the struggle about who will be more effective in counteracting the excesses of global capitalism—Third Way multiculturalist tolerance or populist homo-phobia. Will this boring alternative be Europe's answer to globalisation? Berlusconi is thus post-politics at its worst; even *The Economist*, the staunch voice of anti-left liberalism, was accused by Berlusconi of being part of a 'communist plot', when it asked some critical questions about how a person convicted of crimes could become the prime minister! What this means is that, for Berlusconi, all opposition to his post-politics is rooted in a 'communist plot'. And in a way he *is* right—this *is* the only true opposition. All others—liberals or Third Way leftists—are basically playing the same game as him, only with different coating. And the hope must be that Berlusconi will also be right with regard to the second aspect of his paranoiac cognitive mapping—that his victory will give an impetus to the real radical left.

Notes

1   Quoted from N Harding, *Leninism* (Durham, 1996), p168.
2   Ibid, p146.
3   I owe this point to Alan Shandro's contribution, 'Lenin and the Logic of Hegemony', at the symposium 'The Retrieval of Lenin', Essen, 2-4 February 2001.
4   John le Carré, 'My Vote? I Would Like to Punish Blair', interview with David Hare in *The Daily Telegraph*, 17 May 2001, p23.
5   Ibid.

Leninism in the 21st century

JOHN REES

Lenin's theory of the party is one of the most disputed questions on the left, certainly since the Bolshevik Revolution, and it is one of the most important in terms of how the left is organising around current anti-capitalist and industrial struggles. It is also a central issue in the political debates about creating a socialist alternative to Labourism.

One of the most common misapprehensions about the revolutionary party is that it is something imposed on the working class from the outside. The picture is that a group of ideologues get together, form a party and, using the most undemocratic means, impose their will on the rest of the working class movement. In fact, properly understood, Lenin's theory of the party implies exactly the opposite. Its necessity emerges out of the very nature of working class struggle. There is a central feature of working class resistance to the capitalist system which demands that we understand how some of us can organise to strengthen the organisation and consciousness of the whole class.

The fundamental issue here, and an issue that Lenin confronted very early on, is the way in which the struggle against the system is inherently uneven. Different groups of workers, at different times, with different sets of ideas, move into struggle against the system. This is the problem of uneven consciousness in the working class movement. If life were simpler, if the ruling class lined up their forces on one side and workers lined up on the other side, perhaps no further discussion of political organisation would be necessary. But this is not how the class struggle works. Everywhere we look we see, instead of neat regimentation, a hugely differentiated field of battle. There are the discontinuities of time—periods of intense class conflict are followed by periods of quietude. There are discontinuities in the type of struggle that takes place—some are economic, others political and still others ideological, to name only the three broad categories in Engels' famous formulation. Then there are the discontinuities between different sections of the working class—different traditions, conflicting working class ideologies, varying levels of consciousness, confidence and combativity and so on. The battles are many and diverse. Workers have varying strengths and weaknesses, can win or be defeated, can generalise in different directions and come to different conclusions. Finally, there are the discontinuities between the working class and other sections of society that may find themselves opposed to the capitalist system—for instance peasants, sections of the petty bourgeoisie, oppressed nationalities.

All this presents any socialist—Leninist or not—with a particular problem: how is it that we can develop organisations within the working class that can relate to this fundamental fact about working class struggle?

There is of course a traditional response within the working class movement, a response which has as long a tradition as, if not longer than, Leninism: the Labour Party in this country and reformist parties internationally. The notion here is that the party represents the class in its totality—that every strand of opinion within the working class should be represented within the organisation. The goal of such organisations is to alter the condition of the working class using the institutions provided by the system—the parliamentary system, local councils, etc. The fundamental difficulty with such an approach (and we can review the history of Labour governments in office to justify this claim) is that, so long as the system continues to dominate the lives and the ideas of workers, the organisation itself will end up reflecting the ideology of the system. It will turn from an organisation of resistance to an organisation of incorporation. Moreover, the political institutions of the capitalist system are incapable of effectively countering the political and economic power of the capitalist class.

Of course contradictions will arise between the interests of working class supporters and the limits imposed on such parties by their form of organisation and their political goals. There will be battles for the soul of such organisations, but this will be a continuous state, as it has been for the Labour Party. Sometimes they will move to the left, sometimes to the right. But they will never resolve these contradictions because in principle they attempt to represent the whole working class, and large sections of the working class, for long periods of time, reflect the dominant ideology of society—the ideology of the capitalist class.

We need an alternative view of how party organisation relates to the broader struggle of the working class. It is this idea more than any other with which Lenin's name is associated. The basic conception is that there emerges from the working class struggle a militant minority that is convinced by its experience that the system has to be transformed as a whole, that the direct methods of struggle employed by the working class are the most efficacious methods of doing so, and that the party and the class must be universal—in Lenin's words, the tribune of the oppressed.

The key question then becomes, how do we organise a minority so that they become the lever which can raise the combativity of the entire class? We don't seek to simply 'represent' the class, but to represent the traditions of struggle, the high points of class struggle, and bring that experience together with the activity of the minority into the current struggles. Trotsky expressed this idea in an effective metaphor. He said that the first five workers that he met told him everything he needed to know about revolutionary organisation. There was one who was always militant, would always stand up for the oppressed, and was always at the forefront of any battle. There was one who was an out and out reactionary, who was born a scab and would die a scab—if there were a strike on the gates of heaven he'd scab on that. But there were three in the middle who could sometimes be influenced by the reactionary, and sometimes be influenced and won over by the militant. The purpose of the revolutionary organisation is to group together the one militant in every five workers and to give them the organisation, the strength, the consciousness, the traditions of struggle that would enable them to win over the three in the middle and isolate the right wing, and not to allow the right wing to win over the three in the middle and isolate the socialist.

The idea of an organised minority is not that it cuts itself off from the rest of the working class or imposes its will on them, but that through interaction in struggle with the rest of the working class it seeks to spread its ideas and to win a majority within the movement. Georg Lukács put it very well: we separate in order to unite. We separate in an organisation that is, in principle, opposed to the system, but at every opportunity we seek to unite in particular struggles with the majority of the class in order to advance the whole class struggle. The interaction between party and class is vital here. Lukács quotes Engels thus: rank and file soldiers under the pressure of battle develop all the advances in military tactics. The job of good leadership is not to say that they have all the answers, but to take the best of what is invented by the rank and file in the midst of battle and to generalise it throughout the army. Any revolutionary party that is worth its salt is about learning from people in struggle and generalising what it learns throughout the class. The party learns from the class, but it is also the mechanism by which every section of the class learns from the best experiences of struggle.

This form of organisation is absolutely necessary in the situation in which we now find ourselves. The principle that we stand in opposition to the capitalist system, that we will fight its market logic and the state repression that it entails, is still vital. We need no other argument than the shooting of Carlo Giuliani on the great anti-capitalist demonstration in Genoa in July 2001 to remind us that we still have a state machine that will use deadly force when threatened. But that is only part of it. The real core of this idea of opposition to the system is that it determines how we act in each and every struggle. If you believe, as every Leninist believes, that ordinary working people have the capacity to completely transform the system by democratic organisations, workers' councils, built from the rank and file up, it affects how you treat every day to day struggle.

In every struggle, every strike meeting or campaign meeting, there will always be more than one argument put in the room. There will always be people who will say, 'We don't want to rock the boat. We don't want too big a protest. We should just write to our MP, use the established channels,' and so on. There will be other people, revolutionaries who in principle believe that working people have the capacity to change the system from below, who will argue differently. They will say, 'No matter how small the struggle in which we are engaged, it is mass organisation, it is the involvement of people in demonstrations, it is the ability of people to elect strike committees so that they don't get told what to do by the officials, that can give us the best chance of winning.' It is that principle embodied in each struggle before the revolution which makes the revolutionary principle active in every struggle on the way to the complete transformation of society.

Only an organisation that believes in this end of the day goal will raise this same prospect in each struggle as we go along. When it comes to the recent rail strikes it will be people coming from this tradition who will most consistently raise the idea of picketing, asking for solidarity from other workers, of strikers relying on their own strength and not relying on the trade union leaders, the local MP or the local paper to do the fighting for them. The key question within the anti-capitalist movement is that of mass working class mobilisation as opposed to, on the one hand, compromising with the IMF or WTO or, on the other hand, allowing a small elite of activists to substitute for mass action. When it comes to building an alternative to Labourism, the debate is about how we recompose an alternative to New Labour's neo-liberal agenda from the rank and file up. When it comes to beating the fascists is it enough to allow them freedom of the airwaves and hope that they expose themselves? Is it enough to just pass resolutions? Or do we need the participation of the unions and of rank and file workers to beat the Nazis in Oldham and Burnley?

In all of these cases what is required is one militant, helped by his comrades, supported by his press, to stand up and say, 'No, we all need to do it together.' In that famous scene in the film *Spartacus*, someone stands up first and says, 'I am Spartacus,' not because they could do it on their own—if no one else had stood up after them and said, 'I am Spartacus,' they would have been isolated and victimised—but somebody said it first, and them saying it first allowed everybody else to say it after them. The act of a minority triggers the act of resistance of the majority, and that is what guarantees us the greatest chance of victory.

Redrawing the political map: nationalism, Islamism and socialism in the Middle East

ANNE ALEXANDER

The wave of protests which swept the Arab world in the wake of the Israeli invasion of the West Bank on 29 March 2002 marked a turning point for an entire generation. Demonstrations pulled first thousands, then hundreds of thousands, then finally millions, onto the streets. In country after country rage at the butchery in Ramallah, Bethlehem and Jenin became an explosion of anger at Israel's imperialist backers and their local clients—the Arab regimes. Although several governments tried to channel anger into charity telethons, blood donation campaigns and official demonstrations as the weeks went by,[1] the protest movement was a spontaneous explosion of anger from below. An important article in the Egyptian paper *Al-Ahram Weekly* argued in mid-April:

> The political map, 'stagnant' as it is, seemed until now to consist of the NDP [the ruling nationalist party], *a number of left and right wing parties, and the outlawed Muslim Brotherhood. But when thousands across the nation went out on massive Palestine solidarity, anti-Israeli and anti-American demonstrations over the past three weeks, it began to seem like new and different forces might well be redrawing the map.*[2]

This article attempts to chart the emergence of this movement, and to assess the extent to which the existing political traditions of nationalism and Islamism can offer leadership to the protests. Despite the fact that nationalist and Islamist ideas are the common political language of the solidarity movement, both these currents face profound problems in trying to recreate the successes of their pasts. The dilemmas faced by the mainstream nationalist movements, such as Fatah in Palestine, or the large Islamist groups, such as the Muslim Brotherhood, have not been solved. The economic and political space which allowed such movements to dominate the political map of the Middle East is now more restricted than ever before.

Leon Trotsky's theory of permanent revolution, first written in response to the events of the Russian Revolution of 1905, shows a different route out of the crisis. Although the process of globalisation has reinforced the links between the Arab bourgeoisie and the world ruling class, it has also strengthened the Arab working class. Unless the solidarity movement with Palestine can harness the power of the organised working class, it risks repeating the failures of the nationalist and Islamist movements of the past.

A crucial feature of the demonstrations across the Middle East in solidarity with Palestine was the sheer scale of the movement. On 30 March protests exploded in Cairo, Beirut, Damascus and Amman.[3] Within a couple of days the mainly student-led demonstrations had spread from the capital cities to provincial towns.[4] The first few days of protests were not important simply because of the numbers involved. The largest marches did not take place until the end of the first week of April, and these were in many cases either government approved or called by the major political parties and trade unions. The Syrian state media claimed 1 million people had marched in Damascus on 6 April.[5] Sudanese government ministers addressed the million-strong march in Khartoum,[6] while prominent politicians took part in a similar sized demonstration in Morocco's capital, Rabat, on 7 April.[7] The first protests, although in many cases involving thousands rather than tens of thousands, had a profoundly radicalising effect on the solidarity movement because they emerged outside the framework of official politics. This influence has been most prominent in Egypt and Lebanon, but even in Syria and Saudi Arabia the broad-based solidarity movement has created a new space for political activism.

A new infrastructure of protest

The solidarity protests in Egypt have given birth to a broad popular movement. In addition to the demonstrations, other forms of protest have pulled hundreds of thousands of people into activities in solidarity with the Palestinians. Boycott campaigns targeting Israeli and US goods have been spread by local committees, text messages, internet sites and newspaper adverts. Fatemeh Farag, writing in *Al-Ahram Weekly*, describes the changed atmosphere in Cairo:

Only the other day, my hitherto totally apolitical brother walked in with a huge Palestinian flag, demanding that I hang it from my balcony. In the latest hit by pop singer Mohamed Fouad, he asks God to make him a martyr for Al-Aqsa... Get into a cab and the driver will talk politics and not the traffic. Walk into a cafeteria and your friends are bound to make a fuss if the waiter only has Coke on offer. 'What! You serve products that are on the boycott list!' is the usual rebuke.[8]

Even the state-run media in Egypt was infected by the mood. The main government newspapers, *Al-Akhbar* and *Al-Ahram*, printed extensive reports on the protests in Egypt, including pictures of schoolgirls leading demonstrations in solidarity with the Palestinians.[9] Egyptian president Hosni Mubarak was sufficiently worried by this to call senior editors into his office that week to give them a dressing down for 'endangering national unity'.[10] However, this broad movement has from the very beginning had a sharp political edge. The initial demonstrations were led by students at Cairo University. On 1 April they broke through police lines to lead a large and militant protest in the street. One student was shot dead by police after around 9,000 protesters smashed their way out of the Alexandria University campus on 9 April.[11] A communiqué from the Ministry of the Interior said the trouble started when 'some left wing elements steered demonstrators out of the Alexandria University campus and stoned police forces'.[12] Chants on the demonstrations regularly attack the regime: 'Mubarak, you coward, you are the client of the Americans' and 'We want a new government because we've hit rock bottom' are two favourites.[13] There is also a growing sense that the spontaneous explosion of anger has the potential to develop into a more permanent movement:

Activists speak of a new infrastructure of protest that has grown up since the demonstrations, a network of contacts between student leaders at both Cairo and provincial universities, civil associations involved in the intifada solidarity movement and the professional syndicates. Activists even speak of a geographical centre in the Lawyers' Syndicate, which has opened its doors to students and the public for political seminars, Palestinian nationalist sing-alongs and other events, and is even jokingly called 'Petrograd' in a reference to the Russian Revolution.[14]

In Lebanon a similar infrastructure of protest also emerged during the first few days of the demonstrations. As in Egypt, the independent left, activists from the NGOs and large numbers of school and university students set the pace of the protests. The major student 'sit-in'—an outdoor occupation in Martyrs' Square in downtown Beirut—quickly became an organising centre for many of the most militant actions.[15] The broad coalition, which emerged as the most radical force on the demonstrations, included not only the Palestinian factions and existing left wing groups such as the Communist Party and the Progressive Socialist Party, but also new layers of activists. When, after nearly four weeks, the party activists argued that the time had come to end the sit-in, it was the independents who wanted to stay.[16]

Even Syria, where state-sponsored demonstrations are routine but spontaneous protests very rare, saw the beginnings of a similar process of radicalisation. Pictures of the Syrian president, Bashar al-Asad, were largely absent from the protests of the first few days. Banned left wing organisations were seen leafleting openly on the demonstrations in which the Kurdish groups, Hezbollah, the Nasserist organisations and the Communists were the main organised forces. As well as the usual slogans in solidarity with Palestine, protesters raised chants attacking the government and calling for the release of political prisoners.[17] Saudi Arabia meanwhile has seen an explosion of activism around the campaign to boycott US goods. A Saudi businessman told *Jedda Arab News*:

> *I have never seen such an organised anti-US campaign in the kingdom. It looks as if everyone is involved, from school students to religious scholars. Two days ago, a carefully prepared 20-page file was thrown into my house, containing all the information about the US products we should stop buying. They are well organised.*[18]

The pan-Arab daily *Al-Hayat* described on 6 May how a teacher and students from a girls' college in Jeddah organised a picket of the Doughnut House Company's local restaurant after the company appeared on the boycott list. The company has offered a reward of 1 million Saudi riyals to anyone who can prove that it is not fully Saudi owned.[19] Thousands attempted to march on the US consulate in Dhahran on 12 April.[20] The Palestinian newspaper *Al-Quds al-Arabi* reported on 6 May that during serious disturbances in Sukaka in eastern Saudi Arabia two protesters were arrested for opening fire on riot police.[21]

Arab nationalism reborn?

Although the protests have in general emerged outside the framework of official politics, the language of the demonstrations in solidarity with Palestine has expressed itself through borrowings from the past, as with any new movement. Alongside the bootleg cassettes and smuggled cigarettes in Midan Ataba in Cairo, stalls selling black and white pictures of Gamal Abdul Nasser were doing a roaring trade in the last week of March. Instead of the usual bland mixture of Arab and Western pop, almost every radio in the market was tuned to speeches from the Arab summit in Beirut, while customers in cafes sat mesmerised by live reports from the occupied cities of the West Bank. When protests exploded onto the streets a few days later, many reports were quick to draw parallels with the massive nationalist movements of the 1940s and 1950s. Nasser's old adviser, the former editor of the Egyptian daily paper *Al-Ahram*, Muhammad Hassanain Haikal, appeared on satellite television to argue that the huge protests showed that the ideas of Arab nationalism still dominate the Arab street.[22]

One of the visible signs of the revival of a diffuse kind of Arab nationalism has been the resurrection of Yasser Arafat as a political symbol for the Palestinian struggle. His picture was carried by hundreds of thousands on protests around the Arab world. Here the pan-Arab media has played an important role. Arafat spoke to millions across the Middle East from his candle-lit office under siege in Ramallah. Thanks to the satellite channels, his call—'A million martyrs for Jerusalem!'—echoed through the streets of the Arab capitals. After years of dead-end negotiations and compromise Arafat's Fatah movement seemed to have rediscovered its radical soul. The re-emergence of Fatah has not been confined to the level of symbols. The Al-Aqsa Martyrs Battalions, which are affiliated to Fatah, are by a long way the most active and effective of the Palestinian militia groups. Over the past few years Fatah has rebuilt its organisation in the refugee camps of Lebanon and Syria, reopening offices which were closed and paying for full time organisers once again. *Al-Sharq al-Awsat* reported in June 2001 that Fatah officials had begun to rebuild militia units in Lebanon and were re-establishing military control of the country's Palestinian refugee camps.[23] For the first time in years Fatah and the PLO organised demonstrations of tens of thousands from the camps into central Beirut during the recent protests.[24] The intensification of the intifada, and in particular the rebirth of the guerrilla struggle in Palestine have also helped to revive the fortunes of the other PLO factions, such as the PFLP. For the first time in 30 years the PFLP-General Command (a split from the main PFLP) brought thousands of Palestinian refugees out of the camps in Syria onto the streets of Damascus.[25]

Yet the lifting of the siege on Ramallah shows that Arafat is still vulnerable. His desperate need to achieve a deal with the US and Israel to allow him to rebuild the Palestinian Authority has undermined his newfound popularity among both Palestinians and the wider solidarity movement. Peter Ford, writing in *Al-Sharq al-Awsat*, argued on 5 May that Arafat had emerged from the siege of Ramallah weaker, while the unity of the Palestinian leadership showed signs of splitting under pressure.[26] Ghassan Shirbil, writing in *Al-Hayat*, argued that Arafat faced his real test as he emerged from the ruins of the Muqat'aa Building in Ramallah:

Every Arab and every Palestinian had hoped that Arafat would emerge from the siege to take up his dual role as President of the Palestinian Authority and leader of the intifada once again... He has left the siege to return to his position as President of the Authority, but in the context of a return to negotiations with all their limitations. This means that the next big question will be the fate of the intifada itself.[27]

At a rally of 40,000 in the Sidi Gaber mosque in Alexandria called by the Egyptian People's Committee for Solidarity with the Intifada on 4 May protesters chanted slogans opposing Arafat's 'sell-out' deal with the US.[28] The Nasserist paper *Al-Arabi* reported that, despite the frantic efforts of the Grand Shaykh to calm the crowd, thousands at prayers in the Al-Azhar Mosque in Cairo began chanting the name of PFLP General Secretary Ahmad Sa'dat, whom Arafat handed over to British and US jailers as the siege ended.[29]

The weight of the past

It is also clear that in a large number of countries the major Islamist parties were not in control of the emerging movement. The Labour Party in Egypt was for many years the legal outlet for the main Islamist movement in the country, the Muslim Brotherhood. Although the Brotherhood and the Labour Party are now illegal, the Islamists constitute the major force within the Egyptian opposition to the Mubarak regime. Magdi Hussein from the Labour Party told *Al-Ahram Weekly*:

The Brotherhood didn't really participate in the demonstrations that we, as national political movements, organised. They've always maintained a static rather than dynamic posture, which is to maintain their organisational presence and not clash with the government. So even if there is a need to take action, as the situation entails now, the Brotherhood doesn't take action.[30]

The Muslim Brotherhood in Jordan is even stronger than in Egypt. For many years it was the only major political force outside the regime, and some of its leading members have served in recent Jordanian governments. Yet it neither initiated nor fully controlled the recent protests. After several days of militant student demonstrations, the government effectively made a plea to the Brotherhood to step in and take over the movement, in order to rein it in. The interior ministry gave permission for a large demonstration, which was led off by senior government officials. However, this failed to halt the protests, and the Brotherhood called a demonstration in conjunction with the rest of the opposition and several trade unions for 12 April after Friday prayers. The government then switched tack and banned the march.[31] Troops and tanks moved into

Amman to stop protesters assembling and the government gave a clear signal that it was prepared to use force to crush the demonstration. At the last minute the Brotherhood backed down from a head-on collision with the government and cancelled the demonstration.[32]

Both the nationalist and Islamist movements are weighed down by a long history of failure. The current corrupt, repressive regimes in Syria, Iraq, Egypt and Algeria are the direct successors of the national liberation movements of the 1950s and 1960s. Nationalist parties are still either completely subsumed by the state or represent only a tiny oppositional force. The contradictions of these movements are probably best expressed by the Palestinian national liberation movement which, unlike its counterparts in Egypt, Syria, Iraq and Algeria, still has unfinished business with its colonial oppressors. Despite the acute crisis over Palestine, Arafat and the leadership of Fatah see no other strategy than continual compromise with Israel and the US. Israel's overwhelming military superiority means that the Palestinian national liberation movement has only been able to create at best a stunted bantustan of a state. In order to start building this Palestinian state in the West Bank and Gaza, the PLO accepted a peace deal with Israel which made the fulfilment of even the basic national demands of Palestinian people impossible. The Oslo accords offered neither sovereignty nor prosperity to the Palestinians, let alone justice and democracy. Although the infrastructure of the Palestinian state is now buried under the mangled ruins of Ramallah, Yasser Arafat is still prepared to compromise with the US by trying members of the PFLP for the assassination of the Israeli minister of tourism, Rehavam Ze'evi.

As for the Islamists, they too are an old movement. The revolution in Iran has long lost its radical edge—the Iranian ruling class is currently engaged in a lengthy public debate about whether to recognise the US. Members of the Muslim Brotherhood have served in the cabinet in Jordan, while the Islamists in Algeria briefly controlled local government. Even Hezbollah is not immune to the pressure of events. Ironically, the organisation's success in liberating the south of Lebanon from Israeli occupation has brought new pressures. Increasingly Hezbollah has faced demands to intervene in defence of Shi'ite workers' struggles, for example during the occupation of Middle East Airlines in 2001 and in a recent taxi drivers' strike in Beirut.[33] If the economic crisis in Lebanon deepens, Hezbollah is likely to find itself trapped between the demands of the Lebanese ruling class that it restrict its activities to the south, and pressure from below to defend the interests of the hundreds of thousands of Lebanese who support the movement.

Permanent revolution in the Middle East

The gap between rhetoric and reality is not just a temporary result of organisational frailty. There are much broader reasons why neither the nationalist nor Islamist movements of the Middle East can offer effective leadership to the emerging mass movement in solidarity with Palestine, let alone address the deeper social and economic crisis developing across the region. The organisations where the contradictions are most acute, such as Fatah in Palestine and the Muslim Brotherhood in Jordan and Egypt, have been tied to sections of the bourgeoisie for decades. Fatah was founded by Palestinians who had made fortunes in the Gulf during the boom years of the 1960s—most famously Yasser Arafat himself—and has always looked towards some of the most politically conservative sections of the Arab bourgeoisie for support.[34] These are precisely the layers within the Arab bourgeoisie which have the most to lose from a confrontation with Israel, and by extension the US, and the most to gain from a negotiated settlement. Fatah's backers have long been incapable of challenging US domination of the Middle East. The Brotherhood in Egypt developed a symbiotic relationship with sections of the Egyptian ruling class. Figures such as Uthman Ahmad Uthman, founder of the Arab Contracting Co, channelled profits from the Gulf construction boom of the 1970s back to the Brotherhood, and served as a link with sections of the Sadat regime.[35] This organic connection to Egyptian capital has reinforced the Brotherhood's reformist orientation. As the Egyptian state has given ground to Islamist demands for the 'Islamisation' of law and government, the Brotherhood's leadership has become ever more careful to avoid confrontation with the regime.

The more radical Islamist and nationalist movements have traditionally looked to a thin layer of radical middle class intellectuals as the driving force for social change.[36] Thus the PFLP, although it appeals to 'the masses', relies in practice on the armed struggle of a minority to achieve liberation for Palestine.[37] Islamic Jihad in Palestine argues for an Islamist version of the same strategy—Islamic Palestine will be created by the revolutionary struggle of an armed minority against Israeli occupation.[38] Hamas and Hezbollah combine some of the features of the Muslim Brotherhood, such their links to either state patronage or conservative Gulf capital, with features of the radical nationalist and Islamist groups, in particular their stress on the centrality of the armed struggle and their radical criticisms of the mainstream Palestinian nationalist movement.[39] For both the radical and mainstream nationalists and Islamists the role of the state is crucial. The Arab nationalist leaders of the 1950s and the Islamist clergy of Iran after 1979 attempted to use the state to overcome the uneven and contradictory nature of economic development in the Middle East. The conservative Islamist movements such as the Muslim Brotherhood measure their success by how far they have managed to influence the state from within.

The nationalists of the 1950s won the support of millions of ordinary people by promising that the entire nation could benefit from economic growth, not simply a privileged minority. Islamist rhetoric about a just Islamic economic order has the same kind of appeal today. In the 1950s that meant breaking the power of European colonialism. Today's nationalists and Islamists stress the need to complete the process of national liberation in Palestine and to destroy US economic and military domination of the entire region.

In the early 20th century socialists in Russia faced a very similar set of economic and political problems. Russian capitalism had developed late. Advanced industry existed side by side with a countryside still racked by catastrophic famines. Foreign capital dominated the Russian economy—investors from Western Europe made huge profits while the Tsarist autocracy used savage repression against calls for democracy and basic civil rights.[40] Russian socialists expected that the first stage of the revolution against the Tsarist state would bring the Russian liberal bourgeoisie to power. Just as in the English and French revolutions of earlier centuries, the Russian bourgeoisie would uproot the decaying feudal system in order to lay the foundations for a capitalist republic.[41] By contrast, the Russian revolutionary Leon Trotsky argued that the Russian bourgeoisie, because it had developed far later than its counterparts in Western Europe, was incapable of carrying out this task. Russia's uneven economic development had created a weak and stunted bourgeoisie, squeezed between the domination of foreign capital on the one hand, and the lingering power of the feudal autocracy on the other, which would not dare challenge for political power.

He also argued that, despite the misery and poverty in the Russian countryside, the peasantry could not take independent action in place of the bourgeoisie. Yet the acute social contradictions in the Russian countryside could not be solved unless the Russian Revolution broke down the entire system of bourgeois property relations. The young and small working class was therefore the only class which could play this revolutionary role.[42] However, although what Trotsky called 'the privilege of backwardness' made late developing capitalist economies more vulnerable to overthrow from below, the same underdevelopment meant that attempts to construct a socialist society on such impoverished soil were bound to fail. Without revolutions in the heartland of advanced capitalism the Russian Revolution would collapse. Trotsky argued that the completion of the socialist revolution 'within national limits is unthinkable...the socialist revolution becomes a permanent revolution in a newer and broader sense of the word; it attains completion only in the final victory of the new society on our entire planet'.[43]

By the mid-20th century many features of Trotsky's analysis of Russian society could be applied across the Middle East. The central question in the Arab world was not simply the overthrow of feudalism as it had been in Russia, but also the expulsion of the colonial powers. As in Russia, one of the obstacles to achieving both the democratic revolution and national liberation was the cowardly nature of the Arab bourgeoisie. In Egypt, for instance, although the native capitalist class was constrained by the British presence, it had neither the strength nor the inclination to challenge the occupiers directly. During the post-war period the major nationalist party, the Wafd, played a marginal role in the national liberation movement. Both the industrial bourgeoisie and the rural landowners who supported the Wafd feared the rising workers' movement and the spectre of peasant revolution far more than they feared the British.[44]

Trotsky's prediction that the working class would play the central role in smashing the old system was also confirmed. The driving force behind the mass protests and strikes which broke the British occupation in Egypt was the alliance between the student movement and the independent trade unions. The textile workers of Shubra al-Khayma in Cairo, Mahalla al-Kubra in the Delta and Kafr al-Dawwar were the heart of the nationalist movement of the 1940s.[45] In Iraq in 1958 the workers' movement played a similar role in bringing down the British-backed monarchy.[46] The same process was at work during the Iranian Revolution of 1979. The organised working class played a vital role in smashing the rule of the Shah.[47]

Yet neither Egypt in the 1940s nor Iran in the 1970s confirmed the final part of Trotsky's prediction—the victory of the working class. The contradiction between workers' participation in the national liberation movements and the actual nature of the regimes they produced was profoundly disorientating for a generation of socialists across the Middle East. The Stalinist Communist parties, like some sections of the Russian socialist movement in the early 20th century, argued that the working class could not seize power while the national revolution was incomplete. The leadership of the national liberation movement had to come from the bourgeoisie—and if the big bourgeoisie was too weak to challenge colonialism, the Communists argued that the decisive role fell on the nationalist intelligentsia or radical army officers.[48] It was just such a small group of army officers, led by Gamal Abdul Nasser, who seized power in Egypt in 1952. The Free Officers regime moved quickly to smash the independent workers' movement—trade unions were incorporated into the state and strikes were banned. The Stalinist Communist movement supported the Free Officers coup, and even backed the regime's attack on the workers' movement—in the interest of completing the 'national revolution'.[49] In Iraq ten years later the Communist parties argued that the class interests of workers had to come second to the demands of national unity.

In an important reassessment of Trotsky's theory, Tony Cliff argued that the problem was that, although 'the conservative, cowardly nature of a late developing bourgeoisie is an absolute law, the revolutionary character of the young working class is neither absolute nor inevitable'. This meant that if the working class movement lacked the independent political leadership of a mass revolutionary party, other forces could win state power. Cliff's analysis centred on the experience of revolution in China and Cuba, where intellectuals had led successful peasant guerrilla movements to seize control of the state. He argued that where the working class was passive, or a mass revolutionary party was lacking, nationalist movements could use the state to accelerate industrial development following the model of Stalinist Russia.[50]

Events in Iran in 1979 demonstrated once again that in the absence of a revolutionary party workers could play a leading role in a revolutionary crisis but still not benefit from the outcome. The uprising which overthrew the repressive US-backed regime of the Shah involved factory occupations, general strikes and a mass workers' movement. Until a relatively late stage the radical clerics around Ayatollah Khomeni played a marginal role. Yet, partly because the Iranian left did not offer any independent leadership to the workers' movements, Khomeni and the Islamist clergy were able to seize power and turn the full force of the state against the organised working class.[51] They were also able to fulfil a role similar to the nationalist leaders of a previous generation in reorganising Iranian capital. As Chris Harman puts it, the Islamist clergy were not:

> *as many left wing commentators have mistakenly believed, merely an expression of 'backward' bazaar-based traditional, 'parasitic', 'merchant capital'. Nor were they simply an expression of classic bourgeois counter-revolution. They undertook a revolutionary reorganisation of ownership and control of capital within Iran even while leaving capitalist relations of production intact, putting large scale capital that had been owned by the group around the Shah into the hands of the state and parastate bodies controlled by themselves—in the interests of the 'oppressed' of course.[52]*

The success of the nationalist and Islamist movements of the past in seizing control of the state, and using it as vehicle for economic development and national liberation, does not mean that their 21st century successors can easily use the same methods to solve the problems of the Middle East today. The economic and political space in which these movements now operate is far more constricted.

Since the end of the long boom in the late 1960s there has not been enough slack in the world economy to make the path of independent state capitalist development a practical option for the majority of Third World countries. Rather than funding infrastructure projects as they did in the 1960s, international financial institutions such as the World Bank and International Monetary Fund have for the past 25 years only rewarded governments which cut their expenditure and seek to reduce state intervention in the economy. With the demise of the Soviet Union, Third World governments seem to have little choice but to submit to the demands of IMF-style 'structural adjustment'. The increasing internationalisation of trade and production favours the strong rather than the weak. Thus only small sections of local capital in the Middle East, usually those closest to the state, have been able to benefit from globalisation. This select few have won lucrative franchises from the multinationals to produce brand name consumer goods and services, which only a tiny minority can afford. In the meantime the vast majority are facing job losses, disintegrating basic services, and spiralling prices and rents.[53]

There have always been limits on the ability of any individual state to seriously challenge the imperialist powers or to develop the national economy in order to raise living standards for the mass of ordinary people. In the context of a world economic crisis these two goals become almost impossible to achieve. This is why the national liberation movements which came to power late have moved ever more quickly to find an accommodation with imperialism. The PLO was not alone in making 'historic compromises' during the 1990s. The Republican movement in Northern Ireland also embarked on a peace process. Even those national liberation movements which came to power on a wave of mass struggle, such as the ANC in South Africa, quickly found that, although the old rulers had been forced to give up formal political control, they retained their economic dominance.

Fifty years after Nasser took power in Egypt and nearly a century after the 1905 revolution in Russia, we have come full circle, back to Trotsky's theory of permanent revolution. The only force which is capable of achieving either a democratic revolution against the Arab regimes or national liberation for Palestine is the working class. The Arab bourgeoisie, tied as it is to imperialism, and increasingly integrated into the world ruling class—albeit two or three rungs below the rulers of Europe, North America or Japan—has long ceased to be a force for change.

Just as the process of globalisation has speeded up the integration of the local ruling classes of the Middle East into the world economy, so too it has increased the size and weight of the urban and rural working class. The peasant economy of the countryside is a distant memory. The Egyptian government recently dismantled the reforms of the 1950s and 1960s which allowed a limited redistribution of land in order to open the countryside up to investment from multinational agribusinesses.[54] The result has been to force hundreds of thousands of small peasant farmers off the land. Meanwhile white collar public sector workers have also seen their living standards slide over the past two decades. A job in state bureaucracy used to offer a relatively secure future. Now many office workers are paid less than factory workers. Syrian economists calculated that even those public sector workers with a higher university degree do not earn enough to feed a family.[55] This relentless pressure on the peasantry and the middle class increases both the social weight of the working class and the importance of its political role.

Previous mass movements against imperialism in the Middle East have demonstrated that general political radicalisation over the question of national liberation can feed into the confidence of the workers' movement. This dynamic has the potential to raise both the tempo of the industrial struggle, and to create a more powerful anti-imperialist movement. Millions of people across the Middle East understand perfectly well that McDonald's is part of the same system as the arms manufacturer McDonnell-Douglas, and that Israel's war on the Palestinians is fought in large part to defend the interests of both. However, a boycott of US multinationals will have a limited effect, while Egyptian firms sell cement to build Zionist settlements in the West Bank, or the Egyptian government agrees to supply Israel with natural gas.[56] The boycott campaigns in Saudi Arabia have shown how difficult it is in today's global economy to disentangle national and international capital.

The conditions for an explosive upturn in the class struggle exist in a number of countries around the region. In Lebanon the last few months have seen a rising number of strikes by public sector workers, and the government is preparing for what will be a major battle to privatise Electricite du Liban, the national power supply company, which employs around 20,000 workers. In addition the price rises caused by the imposition of VAT in February sparked a huge confrontation between the government and the trade union movement including massive demonstrations and a threatened general strike.[57] Although the trade union leaders promptly came to a compromise and called off the strike, the scale of the protest movement showed that generalised discontent can very quickly rise to the surface. The Jordanian government recently renewed a three-year IMF restructuring programme, including the introduction of a sales tax which pushed up the cost of basic goods overnight.[58] The Egyptian economy had to be bailed out once again by a massive injection of cash from the international donors in February. Despite international aid the Egyptian economy is still extremely vulnerable to external economic shock.[59] The complete failure of Hosni Mubarak's government to do anything to support the Palestinians only adds to the unpopularity of the regime. The mass solidarity movement with Palestine has greatly sharpened the social tensions in all these countries, despite the efforts of the regimes to control the protests.

However, the fact that these objective conditions exist does not mean the working class can automatically play the role that Trotsky expected it would. Without the independent leadership of a mass revolutionary socialist party, workers' movements on their own do not guarantee victory for the working class. The emerging forces of the left in the Middle East have to immerse themselves in the mass movements of the day. Unless socialists are at the centre of events they will remain trapped in isolated sects. Building a mass movement accelerates the process of political radicalisation. Lessons which were learnt in years of abstract discussion can be absorbed in the space of a few weeks by new activists. At the same time, however, socialists have to argue that building an independent revolutionary party is the best way to ensure the ultimate victory of those mass movements. Such a party cannot be a replica of the old Stalinist Communist parties of the region—it will have to reject the idea that the fate of the Arab working class can be mortgaged to the Arab regimes, nor even to their more radical nationalist critics.

The concept of a revolutionary socialist party based on the power of the international working class cuts through the idea that somehow liberation can be achieved within the confines of the nation state. Socialism has never been achieved within one country, and the idea that it could be has always been, as Cliff put it, 'a narrow reactionary dream'.[60] Thus it is not enough simply to attack the US or European capitalist class without leading the struggle against their local representatives—such as the Bahgat Group and Orascom in Egypt, or Rafiq al-Hariri's business empire in Lebanon. It is also not enough for revolutionary socialists in the Middle East to call for the liberation of Palestine—they have to actually build an organisation which brings the fight against imperialism into every factory and office, and brings the working class into the fight against imperialism. Only a revolutionary party whose members are, in Lenin's words, not merely trade union secretaries but 'tribunes of all the oppressed people', who would 'react to every manifestation of tyranny and oppression, no matter where it appears, no matter what stratum or class of the people it affects'.[61] For the first time in a generation, the audience for these ideas is no longer confined to a tiny minority. The radicalisation over Palestine has opened up a space in the political map of the Middle East which has been closed for decades. Experience from the past shows that, unless revolutionary socialists show how the organised working class can fill that space, other forces will take their place.

Notes

1   For example, the Egyptian president's wife, Suzanne Mubarak, led a convoy of relief trucks to the Egyptian border with the Gaza Strip. This was greeted with a great fanfare by the state-run Egyptian media, although the Egyptian Popular Committee for Solidarity With the Intifada has been organising similar convoys for the past 18 months. For coverage of the officially-sanctioned convoy see D Hammouda, 'Border March', *Al-Ahram Weekly*, 2-8 May 2002, and 'First Lady Leads Huge Popular March to Rafah in Support of the Palestinian People', *Al-Ahram*, April 2002, p1.

2   A Howeidy, 'A New Political Map?', *Al-Ahram Weekly*, 18-24 April 2002.

3   See, for example, *Al-Ahram*, Cairo, 2 April 2002, and *Jordan Times*, Amman, April 2002.

4   *Al-Ahram* reported on 2 April that demonstrations had spread to Cairo University, Helwan University, the American University in Cairo, Sixth October University, Ain Shams University, and outside the greater Cairo area to Port Said, Minya, Tanta, Al-Arish, Suez, Sohag and Assyut. The *Jordan Times* on the same day described a general strike in Amman, and reported that shops and offices were closed in Karak, Zarqa and Irbid.

5   Syrian Arab News Agency, Damascus, 7 April 2002.

6   *Al-Hayat*, 9 May 2002.

7   T Zemmouri, 'Un si proche Orient', *Jeune Afrique/l'Intelligent*, 15-21 April 2002, p25.

8   F Farag, 'The Many Faces of Solidarity', *Al-Ahram Weekly*, 2-8 May 2002,

9   See, for instance, *Al-Akhbar*, 3 April 2002, and *Al-Ahram*, 3 April 2002.

10   *Middle East News Agency*, 4 April 2002.

11   P Schemm, 'Sparks of Activist Spirit in Egypt', MERIP Press Information Note 90, 13 April 2002, www.merip.org

12   *MENA*, 9 April 2002.

13   P Schemm, op cit.

14   S Negus, 'Apathy on the Wane?', *Middle East International*, 3 May 2002, p24.

15   J Quilty, 'Convulsed over Palestine', *Middle East International*, 19 April 2002, p14.

16   *Al-Safir*, Beirut, 3 May 2002.

17   'Civil Society Wakes Up', *Middle East International*, 19 April 2002.

18   *Jedda Arab News*, 9 May 2002, www.arabnews.com

19   *Al-Hayat*, 6 May 2002.

20   www.aljazeera.net, 12 April 2002.

21   *Al-Quds al-Arabi*, 6 May 2002.

22   A Howeidy, op cit.

23   K Al-Gharby, 'Fatah Moves to Regain Security Control of the Palestinian Camps in Lebanon', *Al-Sharq al-Awsat*, 18 June 2001.

24   *Al-Safir*, Beirut, 30 March 2002.

25   I Hamidy, 'First Demonstration of its Kind for Thirty Years: Syrian Authorities Allow Thousands of Palestinian Refugees to March on the Golan', *Al-Hayat*, 6 April 2002.

26   P Ford, 'After the Siege: A Weakened Arafat Maintains his Popularity in the Face of Israel, International Pressure and Internal Struggles', *Al-Sharq al-Awsat*, 5 May 2002.

27   G Shirbil, 'After the Siege, the Real Test', *Al-Hayat*, 2 May 2002, p5.

28   M Salah, 'Protests in Egypt Oppose Arafat's Policies', *Al-Hayat*, 5 May 2002, p7.

29   J Shahin, '30,000 Protested in Alexandria, Chants Against Arafat in Al-Azhar', *Al-Arabi*, Cairo, 5 May 2002.

30   A Howeidy, op cit.
31   *Al-Ayyam*, Amman, 11 April 2002.
32   M Lynch, 'King Abdullah', MERIP Press Information Note 94, www.merip.org
33   On the MEA strike see A Alexander, 'The Crisis in the Middle East',
      International Socialism 93 (Winter 2001). For a report of the taxi drivers' march
      see H Abdul-Hussain, 'Taxi Drivers March in Protest at Diesel Law', *Daily Star*,
      Beirut, 30 April 2002.
34   P Marshall, *Intifada: Zionism, Imperialism and Palestinian Resistance* (London,
      1989), pp115-127.
35   G Kepel, *The Prophet and Pharoah* (London, 1985), p109.
36   For a full analysis of the Islamist organisations of the Middle East and their
      relationship to the nationalist movements see C Harman, 'The Prophet and the
      Proletariat', *International Socialism* 64 (Autumn 1994), pp3-63. Also on the
      class base of nationalist movements, see C Harman, 'The Return of the National
      Question', *International Socialism* 56 (Autumn 1992), p11.
37   See the PFLP website for English translations of the movement's statements and
      press releases, www.pflp-pal.org
38   See Islamic Jihad's website, www.qudsway.com
39   The Palestine Information Centre carries Hamas's statement and gives detailed
      background information on the movement, www.palestine-info.info
40   L Trotsky, *History of the Russian Revolution* (New York, 1992), ch 1.
41   T Cliff, *Deflected Permanent Revolution* (London, 1986), pp7-8.
42   L Trotsky, op cit, p11.
43   Quoted in T Cliff, op cit, p10.
44   See D Renton and A Alexander, 'Imperialism, Globalisation and Popular
      Resistance in Egypt: 1881-2000', in L Zeilig (ed), *Class Struggle and Resistance
      in Africa* (Bristol, 2002, forthcoming).
45   J Beinin and Z Lockman, *Workers on the Nile: Nationalism, Communism, Islam
      and the Egyptian Working Class 1882-1954* (Princeton, 1987), pp340-342.
46   P Marshall, 'The Children of Stalinism', *International Socialism* 68 (Autumn
      1995), p119.
47   A Bayat, *Workers and Revolution in Iran* (London, 1987), pp100-102. See also M
      Poya, 'Iran 1979', in C Barker (ed), *Revolutionary Rehearsals*, (London, 1987),
      pp123-169.
48   As an internal Communist Party document from the 1950s put it, 'The people's
      democracy we want to establish in Egypt is not a form of the dictatorship of the
      proletariat. We aim to establish a democratic dictatorship if all the classes
      struggling against imperialism and feudalism.' 'CP/CENT/INT/56/03—Note on
      Communist Policy for Egypt', Communist Party Archives, National Museum of
      Labour History, Manchester.
49   See R Bianchi, 'The Corporatization of the Egyptian Labor Movement', *Middle
      East Journal* 40 (1986), pp431-432.
50   T Cliff, op cit, p16
51   P Marshall, op cit, p125.
52   C Harman, op cit, p42.
53   A Alexander, 'The Crisis in the Middle East', op cit, p68.
54   D Renton and A Alexander, op cit.
55   F Al-Khatib, 'Al-Asar wal-Ujur', seminar paper presented at the Syrian
      Economic Society's 'Tuesday Forum', Damascus, 24 April 2001, available on-
      line at http://mafhoum.com/syr/articles_01khatib/khatib.htm
56   *Jerusalem Post*, 5 April 2002.
57   *Daily Star*, Beirut, 13 February 2002, *Al-Safir*, Beirut, 13 February 2002. The
      trade union protests followed large student demonstrations which had brought
      thousands on the streets against budget cuts in the universities. *Al-Safir* reported

that students carried pots and pans, following the example of protesters in Argentina, and banners threatening to carry out an Argentine-style popular uprising if the government refused to listen to their demands. *Al-Safir*, Beirut, 5 February 2002.

58   *Jordan Times*, Amman, 11 March 2002 and *Al-Arab Al-Yawm*, Amman, 17 April 2002.
59   G Essam El-Din, 'Shock-Absorbent Economy?', *Al-Ahram Weekly*, 9-15 May 2002.
60   T Cliff, op cit, p10.
61   V Lenin, 'What is to be Done? Burning Questions of Our Movement', in V Lenin, *Collected Works*, vol 5 (Beijing, 1961), pp422-423.

Islam and imperialism

A review of Tariq Ali, **The Clash of Fundamentalisms: Crusades, Jihads and Modernity** *(Verso, 2002), £15*

SAM ASHMAN

You know how many people they've killed in Central America? You know?…
I feel sorry for the ones who died. That's more than they feel for us.[1]

That is what a Latino taxi driver in New York told Tariq Ali shortly after 11 September when 3,000 died, and when 'the world media, which cast their own discreeter veil over the daily violence in other parts of the world thus rendering it invisible, were drawn straight to the site of the outrage'. For those who opposed the US's revenge bombing of Afghanistan it was never about denying the suffering of those who died in the twin towers. It was more a question of asserting that those who died beneath US and British bombs also suffered, and they suffered at the hands of a far mightier foe. Tariq Ali's new book about Islam, which is really a collection of articles, takes up many of the questions raised across the globe in the wake of 11 September. It is a patchwork analysis, sewn together with personal reminiscences, interesting ideas and, crucially, opposition to imperialism. Towards the end is a chapter called 'A Short-Course History of US Imperialism', which in many ways is the point of departure which informs the whole. Tariq Ali's book conveys three things. Firstly, neither Islam, Christianity nor Judaism has spawned cultures, civilisations or ideas which are monolithic or timeless. Secondly, Islam must be understood from a materialist perspective which understands class and the development of capitalism and imperialism. Thirdly, when we look at the world today the 'mother of all fundamentalisms' is US imperialism.

He is well qualified for the job. Tariq Ali writes as a veteran opponent of US imperialism and hails from a Muslim background of sorts, given that he was born in Lahore when it was under British imperial rule and shortly before it became part of Pakistan. His family, as he tells us, were privileged landowners, his grandfather a leader of the landlords' Unionist Party and governor of the Punjab, his parents members of the Communist Party. When he tells stories of bumping into relatives or family acquaintances they are generals or ambassadors or such like — and he even has one uncle, a Pakistani general, with a very interesting interpretation of Marxist historian Isaac Deutscher's three-volume biography of Trotsky.

The Clash of Fundamentalisms deals with the origins of Islam and the rise and fall of Islamic empires. There is doubtless much that is controversial in his short treatment, but he stresses both the diversity of Islamic traditions and their interrelationship with other traditions. The book traces how the Islamic world expanded to encompass Syria, Egypt and Iraq and then moved westward to conquer northern Africa and Spain, and eastward to conquer India. The conquest of Syria and Persia resulted in a cultural synthesis which produced a new Islamic civilisation absorbing arts, literature and philosophy. Gondeshapur in south west Persia became a centre for intellectuals, dissidents and free thinkers and the development of the philosophy of medicine, while Cordoba in Spain was notorious for dissenters and sceptics. Throughout the Middle Ages the Islamic world preserved ancient Greek thought, providing a bridge to the Renaissance. Poets, philosophers and heretics 'expanded the frontiers of debate' and some even questioned — before the European Renaissance — the oppression of women within Islam.

Later the Islamic Ottoman Empire opened up a new front in south eastern Europe — including Hungary, the Balkans, parts of Ukraine and Poland. By the 15th and 16th centuries the majority of Muslims lived under either the Ottoman Empire or the Mughal Empire in India. These societies, however, did not create capitalist relations of production and ultimately could not withstand the rise of Western capitalism. Tariq Ali writes that:

> ...in very different local conditions, the caliphates in Cordoba, Baghdad, Cairo and Istanbul, and later the Mughal empire in India, did not favour the creation of a landed gentry or peasant ownership or village communities. Either would have aided capital formation, which might later have led to industrialisation.[2]

The Mughal Empire was replaced by British imperialism. Direct rule was imposed following the mutiny of 1857, but merchant capital, in the form of the East India Company, had blazed the trail, and its offices in

London are described as 'the first headquarters of globalisation'. Defeat in the First World War marked the end of the Ottoman Empire which had joined the Austro-German alliance. The victorious powers in that war agreed that the Ottoman Arab states would be given formal independence, but under their 'mandate'. Britain oversaw Iraq, Palestine and Eygpt. France did the same to Syria, the Lebanon, and the Maghreb. Rebellions in Iraq and Syria were crushed almost immediately.

Imperial influence spread to those areas which were not formally mandates or protectorates. Here the treatment of Wahhabism in Saudi Arabia—Osama Bin Laden's home state—is one of the book's strengths. Wahhabism is a branch of Islam, and the official religion of Saudi Arabia and its ruling dynasty—one of the most repressive in the world, let alone the Middle East, but nonetheless a key US ally today because it guards 25 percent of the world's oil reserves. It was inspired by the 18th century preacher Muhammad Ibn Abdul Wahhab, who sought a return to a mythical pure age of Islam. His philosophy only became a material force when Wahhab joined forces with a local emir and bandit, Muhammad Ibn Saud, who sought to rule over neighbouring tribes and to unite the Arabian peninsula which was then a remote and neglected outpost of the Ottoman Empire. The two formed a pact, and by the start of the 19th century Ibn Saud's forces had taken control of a string of cities including the holy sites of Mecca and Medina. The rebellion was eventually crushed by Ottoman forces and the Wahhabis were pushed back to their home base, the Nejd. The story did not end there, however. After the collapse of the Ottoman Empire the emir of the Nejd, one of Ibn Saud's descendants, became a convenient British client ruler. Saudi Arabia was formed in 1927 and US oil companies moved into the country in the 1930s—critically altering the balance of imperial power in the region. They and the ruling Saudi Wahhabis have been together ever since, the Wahhabi royals protecting oil supplies and providing a bulwark against Communism and secular nationalism. Tariq Ali writes, 'The expeditionary force dispatched to Afghanistan to cut off the tentacles of the Wahhabi octopus may or may not succeed, but the head is safe and sound in Saudi Arabia, guarding the oil wells, growing new arms, and protected by American soldiers and the USAF base in Dhahran.'

Another strength of *The Clash of Fundamentalisms* is the way the analysis of events following the end of the Second World War brings together two areas of the world that are generally treated separately—the Middle East and South Asia. The violent processes which led to the formation of the states of Israel and Pakistan are described as different but comparable. The partition of India in 1947 left up to 2 million dead and 11 million refugees, and transformed the South Asian subcontinent. The state of Israel was formed a year later, and while the scale of deaths in Palestine was not the same as in South Asia, the Palestinians were left homeless and stateless in refugee camps in Jordan and Syria. Pakistan was supposedly a homeland for Muslims, Israel supposedly a homeland for Jews. Yet in both cases the founding fathers of these states were far removed from religion. Jinnah was an agnostic whisky drinker, while Ben-Gurion and Moshe Dayan were atheists. Religious fundamentalists in both cases were opposed to the formation of these states, though in Pakistan the *Jamaat-e-Islami* soon changed its mind. British imperialism played a central role in the foundation of both states.

The Muslim League would not have won its demand for a separate 'Muslim' state of Pakistan without the British. The league only adopted the demand in 1940 and failed to win mass support for it. In fact large numbers of Muslims looked to the Indian National Congress as it led the fight against British imperial rule. The league was formed by upper class conservative Muslims who pledged their loyalty to the British. This loyalty was especially important during the Second World War — the Congress launched the Quit India campaign but the league remained loyal to the war effort. The league's loyalty was rewarded when the British left in 1947, dividing the subcontinent and making a 'monsoon with red rain'.

The bloodshed did not stop with partition. Revolt, repression and war would lead to the formation of the state of Bangladesh in 1971 from what had been East Pakistan. The battle over the state of Kashmir, still claimed by both India and Pakistan, continues to take many lives.

Zionism was a secular nationalist ideology created in the 19th century by a small group of secular Jews who thought assimilation into European society was impossible and who began to raise money to settle Jews in Palestine. Britain pledged to aid the formation of a Jewish state in Palestine as early as the 1917 Balfour Declaration which was followed by the annexation of Palestine. Britain then created a nominally independent state of Trans-Jordan (which would later become Jordan) from eastern Palestine and kept the rest of Palestine under direct British control to facilitate a Jewish national home. Significant Jewish immigration began soon after. The first Palestinian intifada against this settlement took place between 1936 and 1939 and was crushed by 25,000 British troops, the RAF and the Zionist settlers together. The British then promised the Zionists their own independent state.

Both Israel and Pakistan emerged from these processes as grotesque societies. But while British imperialism was vital for their creation, US imperialism has been vital for their survival. Both became recipients of huge amounts of US aid in the post-war period as Israel became the US's watchdog in the Middle East and Pakistan became the US's Cold War ally in South Asia. The question of Palestine remains a thread which ties the states of the Arab world together. Tariq Ali describes Israel as the only remaining colonial power on the 19th/20th century model. He has even unearthed an interesting personnel overlap: General Zia-ul-Haq, dictator of Pakistan in the late 1970s and 1980s, was involved in the 'Black September' massacre of Palestinians in Jordan in 1970.

The Clash of Fundamentalisms then moves on to give a potted history of the rest of the Middle East. The book deals well with the Iraq-Iran war, Saddam Hussein, sanctions and the continued bombardment of Iraq. I found two weaknesses in his analysis of elsewhere, however. Firstly, the revolution which deposed the Shah of Iran in 1979 is rather badly described as 'a revolt against History, against the Enlightenment, "Euromania", "Westoxification"—against Progress. It was a postmodern Revolution before postmodernism had grown fashionable.' Now there is a large degree of poetic licence being exercised here, and it is certainly right to describe the Iranian regime as practising the 'anti-imperialism of fools'. But the Iranian Revolution was the very opposite of the postmodern and it is a shame not to educate readers about this story. The revolution did not begin as an Islamist revolution to put Khomeini in power. Instead Khomeini succeeded in filling the vacuum that was created following a mass revolt, which after some 18 months of intense struggle, of mass street demonstrations and increasingly of political strike action, toppled the Shah. Elected strike committees took over important factories, and after the Shah fled, *shoras* (councils) spread from factories to offices, colleges and villages. Khomeini's victory over the movement was not assured for many months, and was only completed on the basis of breaking this new democracy.

Secondly, the book shares a theoretical weakness which is evident on the left today—a sort of sentimental nostalgia for the old Soviet Union and to a lesser extent China. These states are seen as 'no-go areas for world capitalism' and bulwarks against US imperialism. So Tariq Ali writes:

> *Even though the Soviet Union had not represented a serious revolutionary threat for many decades, its very existence had given heart to anti-colonial resistance movements in three continents, enabled the Cubans and Vietnamese to resist and survive, armed the ANC in South Africa and provided European social democracy with a platform to wrest some reforms from the various capitalist elites.*[3]

This may be understandable, given the brutality of US imperialism today, but it nonetheless rewrites history. The USSR was an imperialist power in its own right—its disastrous 1979 invasion of Afghanistan being only one example. Afghan Communists, who had built support in the army, took power in Afghanistan through a coup in 1978. They tried to impose change on the villages of Afghanistan — land reform and an improvement in the position of women — but without a mass base of support. They were seen as puppets of the Russians, and resistance soon began in the name of Islam. The Communists responded with mass arrests, torture and the bombing of whole villages. *The Clash of Fundamentalisms* condemns the repression used by this regime but argues that nonetheless 'the PDPA regime had restarted the process of modernisation'. By late 1979 the regime was so hated that it was about to fall. The Soviet Union responded by invading Afghanistan in order to keep the Communists in power and to prevent Islamic rebellion spreading to what were then its Central Asian republics. The invasion meant that even the Communists' supporters in the cities turned against them and towards Islam. Civil servants, many of whom supported the PDPA regime, went on strike against the Soviets. The book rightly points to how the US seized on this situation as part of its Cold War battle with the Soviet Union, funding Islamic resistance via the Pakistani state and using Egyptian and Saudi state intelligence networks. Nonetheless the resistance could win mass support because the mass of the population opposed the Russian invasion. There were two imperialist sides in the Cold War.

These are minor weaknesses, however, in a book that deserves a wide readership. If you are not familiar with the history of the Middle East and South Asia it provides a pacy introduction. If you are, it provides a timely reminder written with some style. More importantly, because Tariq Ali begins from opposition to US imperialism and to racism and inequality, he can conclude the book with a very powerful 'Letter to a Young Muslim'. Here he argues that 'the rise of religion is partially explained by the lack of any other alternative to the universal regime of neo-liberalism', and that the 'fundamentalism of the Empire has no equal today'. This is combined with a challenge to what Islamists have to offer in response — 'a route to the past which, mercifully for the people of the 7th century, never existed'. This approach is critical for the left today, not only if it is to build opposition to racism, imperialism and fascism in Europe, but also if it is to rebuild its roots in the Middle East, South Asia and beyond. For these reasons, this book deserves a very warm welcome.

Notes

1   T Ali, *The Clash of Fundamentalisms: Crusades, Jihads and Modernity* (London, 2002), p292.
2   Ibid, pp47-48.
3   Ibid, p271.

From *tangentopoli* to Genoa

*A review of Paul Ginsborg, **Italy and its Discontents** (Allen Lane, 2001), £25*

MEGAN TRUDELL

The magnificent protests at the G8 summit in Genoa in July 2001 marked a dramatic shift in Italian politics. The barely two month old government headed by media baron Silvio Berlusconi showed its true colours by barricading the citizens of Genoa and protesters out of the centre of the city, intimidating, beating and torturing peaceful demonstrators, and murdering 23 year old Carlo Giuliani.

The brutality and authoritarian stance of Berlusconi's government have been matched by a growing determination and collective anger among large sections of Italian society. In the days and weeks following the G8 protests, hundreds of thousands marched throughout the country.[1] Since then Rome has seen the biggest demonstration in Italian post-war history. Organised by Italy's biggest union, the CGIL, some 3 million demonstrators filled the city on 23 March 2002 to protest against Berlusconi's proposed reform of Article 18—which gives judges the right to reinstate workers who have been sacked without 'just cause'. Berlusconi's sneering remarks that the demonstrators had only come to Rome for the day 'because someone offered them a free trip, a free lunch and a chance to visit the museums' belied the pressure his government is under from a movement that is fusing anti-capitalism with militant trade unionism.[2] Any doubt about the potential for trade union unity against Berlusconi was dispelled during the 16 April general strike, which saw the three main union federations come together to bring 13 million workers out on strike. It is clear that Italy is in one of the most exciting and volatile periods in its history. For that reason alone, although written before Genoa, Paul Ginsborg's monumental volume is welcome. Ginsborg is very much a part of the emerging movement in Italy. He formed an organisation to preserve democracy in the light of Berlusconi's second election victory, and on the day of the general strike he was interviewed by *Newsnight* on the streets of Florence, linking hands with fellow Florentines to form a chain around the city as part of the protests.

Italy and its Discontents follows Ginsborg's classic study of post-war Italy, *A History of Contemporary Italy*, which was written at the end of the 1980s, and Ginsborg has continued the story in the same thoroughly researched, detailed and accessible fashion. His latest volume encompasses Italy's social, political and cultural history from 1980 to 2001. Ginsborg's location of political events in Italian society within wider social and economic changes makes this book essential reading for anyone interested in the background to Berlusconi's rise (and fall and rise) to power and the nature of the movement that opposes him.

Ginsborg's history alternates between tracing the socio-economic changes in Italy over the last 20 years—with chapters on the economy, class, families, culture, the state, corruption and organised crime—and telling the story of the political events which culminated in the 'earthquake' of 1992-1993, in which a combination of factors toppled an entrenched political class which had governed Italy since the end of the war. In just two years, by 1994, the Christian Democrats were a shadow of their former selves, the Socialist Party had ceased to exist, and Berlusconi's *Forza Italia* was born.

The 1980s

The late 1960s and early 1970s were years of social upheaval—Italy's 'long May'—which rocked the Italian ruling class. Aldo Ravelli, one of the head stockbrokers at Milan's stock exchange, is quoted by Ginsborg as recalling, 'Those were the years in which I tested out how long it would take me to escape to Switzerland. I set out from my house in Varese, and got to the frontier on foot'.[3]

The defeat of a major strike at Fiat in 1980 signalled an end to this threat to the employers, and marked the start of a downturn in Italian working class struggle, around the same time as that in Britain. For Ginsborg the 1980s were the decade in which collective action gave way to individualist consumer capitalism and its values, replacing the individual's social and community involvement with an emphasis on the family and acquisition:

On the one hand, a return of the unquestioned acceptance of hierarchy, by the increased power of monopolies and oligopolies, by the new and deleterious influence exercised by commercial television, by a mass passivity in strong contrast to earlier social patterns of mobilisation. On the other, there were distinct signs of the growth of an autonomous and active civil society.[4]

Ginsborg meticulously draws together the various elements underpinning the dramatic collapse of the *pentipartito*—the Christian Democrat (DC)/Socialist Party (PSI) consensus governments.

In the period between 1981 and 1991 Italians elected nine governments. In 1983 the ruling DC, which had dominated Italian official politics since the war, recorded its lowest ever vote in an election—reflecting how badly discredited it was by the scandal revealing government collusion in the secret anti-Communist Masonic lodge P2 (which was to prove so useful to up and coming media magnate Silvio Berlusconi).

Bettino Craxi, leader of the PSI, headed the government from 1983 to 1987, and it is in this period that Berlusconi built his empire. The two were close friends, and Craxi did all he could to stonewall any regulation of television, allowing his crony to amass a fortune now estimated at £14 billion—with assets including the media company Fininvest, 90 percent control over the state media RAI, most Italian daily newspapers and the football club AC Milan.

The DC/PSI stranglehold on Italian politics was consolidated by the collapse of the Communist Party (PCI) in 1989. Following the fall of the Berlin Wall the party split into the *Partito Democratico della Sinistra* (PDS)—remodelled as Italy's New Labour—and *Rifondazione Comunista*, the left of the PCI.

In the absence of coherent opposition, the DC/PSI goverment pursued a neo-liberal agenda—'freeing' Italian capital, granting autonomy to the Bank of Italy, and pushing through cuts in public spending to ensure Italy could meet the Maastricht criteria.

Widespread state corruption, historically endemic in Italy, accelerated during the 1980s, and both the ruling parties were systematically involved in clientism, accepting bribes, and stealing from the public purse. An added ingredient in Italian politics at this time was organised crime. The Mafia thrived thanks to the collusion of sections of the state. Key figures in Italy's various crime families did deals with politicians which guaranteed votes for immunity from prosecution. The 'maxi-trial' against the Mafia, led by independent magistrates Falcone and Borsellino, began in 1987, and threatened to expose the links between politicians and mafiosi. The classic and disturbing image of the interpenetration of the state and the Mafia in this period is that of 'the kiss' between the leader of the

Sicilian Mafia, Salvatore Riina, and the DC politician and seven times prime minister Giulio Andreotti—a mark of respect and a reminder of mutually assured destruction—fascinatingly discussed in Peter Robb's *Midnight in Sicily*.[5]

This combination of revelations of the state's implication in the strategy of tension and the existence of an unofficial secret service, *Gladio*, set up to discredit the left in the 1970s, the rise of the Northern League as an electoral force in previous DC heartlands, and growing public disgust at the corruption, creaking bureaucracy and bribery ensured that the crisis in 1992 was explosive.

Ginsborg illustrates clearly the bitterness with the political system felt by millions of Italians by setting the events leading up to the crisis against wider social shifts. By 1992 there were 6.5 million Italians living in poverty, disproportionately—though not exclusively—concentrated in the south. In Palermo one third of the city's population live below the poverty line. By1995 unemployment among under-25s was 33.3 percent across the country. The higher education system was disorganised and conservative, workers had faced a decade of defeat and the erosion of their conditions, and small businesses were being squeezed. In sharp contrast to the 'values' of individual enrichment pushed by the political class and their business friends, most Italians were not living *la dolce vita*.

The frustration with the established governing parties and cynicism towards the clientism and corruption of the state were reflected in a myriad of ways—including the growth of support for the Northern League especially in 'white' (ie Catholic) strongholds, and in the growth of 'associations', independent unions, cultural and volunteer groups which Ginsborg groups together as 'civil society'.

Tangentopoli

In February 1992 Mario Chiesa, a Socialist politician in Milan, was caught while trying to flush 30 million lire of bribe money down the toilet. When imprisoned, he exposed the system of kickbacks to magistrates, and key political figures including Craxi and Andreotti were placed under investigation in what became known as *tangentopoli* ('kickback city'). Senior managers at Fiat and Olivetti were under investigation, and details of corporate corruption surrounding the merger between the private company Montedison, owned by the Ferruzi Group, and the state petrochemical firm ENI led to the suicides of the presidents of both firms.

A couple of months later the Mafia fought back against the maxi-trial and killed both Falcone and Borsellino, provoking *The Observer* to comment in July 1992 that Italy was 'in a state of war—it has the highest murder rate in the European Community, the most rampant and blatant corruption, an ailing economy, a floundering government, and an anguished and embarrassed population'.[6]

On Black Wednesday the lira was devalued, just before the pound, and the economic crisis prompted yet sharper attacks from the now utterly discredited government, which attempted to privatise the key state-run electricity and petrochemical industries, and attacked public sector conditions. The anguished population fought back—workers struck against austerity measures, 50,000 demonstrated in Milan, and in February 1993 300,000 protested in Rome and burnt effigies of government leaders, denouncing them as robbers. But incredibly, despite the fact that the political system was reeling, the CGIL did a deal with the Italian bosses' confederation, *Confindustria*, and the government, agreeing to abandon the *scala mobile*—the scale linking wage rises to inflation.

In the March 1994 election the two dominant parties of Italian postwar politics were crushed—the PSI managed only 2.2 percent of the vote. Silvio Berlusconi and his newly formed *Forza Italia* party in alliance with the 'post-fascist' Gianfranco Fini's National Alliance (formerly the MSI) and Umberto Bossi's Northern League stepped into the vacuum left by the implosion of the major parties. Berlusconi's first government was short lived—a general strike and the biggest trade union demonstration (until March this year) in Italian history forced him to climb down on attacking pension rights and forced a U-turn on dropping the *tangentopoli* proceedings. In November 1994 he himself was placed under investigation and his coalition collapsed.

Given Berlusconi's record—at the time of the election he was on trial on ten counts including bribing financial police, attempted corruption of magistrates, tax fraud, illegally financing a political party, and breaching anti-trust laws in Spain—it is extraordinary that he could ever have come back from such defeat and formed another government. But just as the corruption and cronyism of the Socialist Party allowed him to build his empire unrestricted, so the weakness of the Olive Tree coalition—led by Romano Prodi, and backed by the heirs of the PCI—which governed from 1996 to 2001, allowed Berlusconi to return.

Across Europe, at the same time, social democratic governments were being elected—Blair in Britain, Jospin in France, and Schröder in Germany—in rejection of Thatcherite policies. And today right wing politicians are benefiting from the disillusionment and betrayal millions of people across Europe feel as those social democratic governments pursue the same pro-business policies.

In Italy, Berlusconi was re-elected as part of this generalised polarisation in European politics, but the fact that he was not in prison at the time is largely due to the craven behaviour of the DS, under the leadership of

Massimo D'Alema, who let Berlusconi off the hook. The Olive Tree government failed to introduce a conflict of interests law reducing the power of magistrates, and did not force through charges against Berlusconi, despite the fact that he had a virtual monopoly over commerical broadcasting—an influence which now extends over the key state-owned television channels. In Ginsborg's words, the social democratic government 'created a culture of indulgence and pardon'.[7]

Civil society

For Ginsborg, the 1992 crisis provided a space for a new Italy to emerge, but he laments the fact that the DS didn't seize the opportunity handed to it, instead allowing *tangentopoli* to fizzle out without drawing out the links between organised crime and the state—even Andreotti was acquitted. The state survived, and has changed little as a result of the seismic events. Yet, although he is disappointed that political parties and the state have not 'democratised' themselves, he is aware that their very resistance to change can contribute to building a momentum from below which has the potential to force the issue.

In the last paragraph of his book Ginsborg holds the Italian population partly responsible for the state of democracy in the country, but also sees it as part of the solution: 'The strength of a democracy in a single country does not depend only upon the capability or the integrity of its ruling elite, but also upon the culture of its families and the energy of its citizens'.[8]

Ginsborg points to the growth of 'civil society' on the ground—the movements in Palermo against the Mafia, the volunteer movement and the growth of environmentalism which all emerged during the 1990s in exasperation at the inability of the state to deliver. As Tom Behan has written, this was the 'background to the social forum movement which exploded just after Genoa'.[9] Ginsborg is positive about these developments, but seems to hold the view, put forward by Michael Hardt and Toni Negri in their book *Empire*, that the working class is merely one aspect of the 'multitude' of groups and networks which form that civil society. So class is seen as 'another' cleavage in Italian society, not the central one.[10] And it is on this question of agency that the weakness at the heart of Ginsborg's book is apparent. He is gloomy about the ability of the working class to offer a collective solution to capitalism. In one of those unfortunate timings which occasionally wrong-foot pessimists, he describes militant trade unionism as being in grave crisis: 'What has disappeared almost entirely is the presence of the trade union movement as a major social and political protagonist'.[11] Just as Andre Gorz utterly underestimated the potential for workers' resistance in 1968, Ginsborg must be wishing he hadn't written those words.

His perspective rests on the belief that the working class has shrunk numerically and in terms of its political weight. White collar workers, who form 32.4 percent of the workforce, concentrated mainly in education, local government and health, are considered by Ginsborg as part of the 'lower middle class'—which allows him to claim that the middle class are the most numerous in Italian society. This sociological sleight of hand seems to support his political conclusion that it is the 'reflexive' or enlightened intellectual middle class who are the key social force for change in Italian society. So in his discussion of the growth of the associations and networks which took place in the 1980s, he argues that 'the critical and "reflexive" middle classes were certainly at the heart of this construction of civil society, but membership was not just limited to them'.[12] It is this stress on sections of the middle class which leads him to see the general strike of 1994 which was instrumental in bringing down Berlusconi's first government as simply one element of equal weight among many, rather than as central in coalescing opposition.

But his political position also means that Ginsborg's explanations for Berlusconi's rise to power—although fascinating—tend to rest much more heavily on machinations in state and parliament than on how these interacted with levels of class struggle, the confusion and absence of leadership on the left, and the failures of social democracy. It also leads to Ginsborg putting his faith very unadvisably in the DS—as if the party which let Berlusconi off the hook when it had the chance to finish him off, and has, in true Blairite fashion, pandered to his every whim, is a likely conduit for the flowering of democracy in the state.

In actual fact, if the measure for judging the relative strength of the working class is that of Marxism, Ginsborg's own figures are grounds for great optimism. Taken together with the 25 percent of industrial workers, the 32.4 percent who work in white collar jobs confirm that the majority of Italian society is working class. By his own figures, the number of those in 'dependent work'—ie not self employed—has risen dramatically from 49.1 percent in 1960 to 71.8 percent in 1992, reflecting both the growth of the working class and the pressure on the petty bourgeoisie.[13]

The growth in Italy's service sector may have given rise to arguments about the death of the working class, but it has also seen the proletarianisation of previously privileged sections, in very similar ways to what we have seen in Britain, and their induction into class struggle—witness the 90,000 bank workers who closed 90 percent of Italy's banks just months after Ginsborg's book was finished.

The social forum movement and the serious initiatives to extend and politicise the movement by *Rifondazione Comunista* are important political and organisational repercussions of the crisis in mainstream politics coupled with the rise in struggle.

Berlusconi's victory and the presence of fascists and right wing nationalists in his government, the neo-liberal axis he has formed with Blair and Aznar, and the explosive revival of collective struggle and working class militancy in Italy are part of the accelerated nature of polarisation across Europe. The haemorrhaging of support for the governing Socialist Party in France, the huge wave of anti-fascist protest that followed the vote gained by Le Pen in the first round of the presidential election in April, and the 26 seats for Pim Fortuyn's List in the Netherlands all express this trend. Criticisms aside, the clarity, rigour and readability of Ginsborg's book make it essential for those wanting to understand modern Italy to grasp how a right wing politician like Berlusconi can emerge, and to learn the lessons—most crucially how the bankruptcy of social democratic parties can give space to the right. It is therefore the urgent task of the left and the movement to develop a leadership capable of directing the energy and anger that are spreading across the continent in a leftward direction.

Notes

Thanks to Jim Wolfreys and Nicki Sellars for comments.

1   For details see T Behan, 'Nothing Can be the Same Again', *International Socialism* 92 (Autumn 2001).
2   Quoted in *The Guardian*, Wednesday 27 March 2002.
3   P Ginsborg, *Italy and its Discontents* (Allen Lane, 2002), p39.
4   Ibid, p96.
5   See P Robb, *Midnight in Sicily* (Hanill Press, 1999).
6   P Ginsborg, op cit, p263.
7   Ibid, p315.
8   Ibid, p325.
9   T Behan, 'Digging at the Roots of Dissent', *Socialist Review*, March 2002.
10 P Ginsborg, op cit, p39.
11 Ibid, p57.
12 Ibid, p96.
13 Ibid, p51.

The Socialist Workers Party is one of an international grouping of socialist organisations:

AUSTRALIA	International Socialists, PO Box A338, Sydney South
AUSTRIA	Linkswende, Postfach 87, 1108 Wien
BRITAIN	Socialist Workers Party, PO Box 82, London E3 3LH
CANADA	International Socialists, PO Box 339, Station E, Toronto, Ontario M6H 4E3
CYPRUS	Ergatiki Demokratia, PO Box 7280, Nicosia
CZECH REPUBLIC	Socialisticka Solidarita, PO Box 1002, 11121 Praha 1
DENMARK	Internationale Socialister, PO Box 5113, 8100 Aarhus C
FINLAND	Sosialistiliitto, PL 288, 00171 Helsinki
GERMANY	Linksruck, Postfach 304 183, 20359 Hamburg
GHANA	International Socialist Organisation, PO Box TF202, Trade Fair, Labadi, Accra
GREECE	Sosialistiko Ergatiko Komma, c/o Workers Solidarity, PO Box 8161, Athens 100 10
HOLLAND	Internationale Socialisten, PO Box 92025, 1090AA Amsterdam
IRELAND	Socialist Workers Party, PO Box 1648, Dublin 8
NEW ZEALAND	Socialist Workers Organization, PO Box 13-685, Auckland
NORWAY	Internasjonale Socialisterr, Postboks 9226, Grønland, 0134 Oslo
POLAND	Pracownicza Demokracja, PO Box 12, 01-900 Warszawa 118
SPAIN	Izquierda Revolucionaria, Apartado 563, 08080 Barcelona
UNITED STATES	Left Turn, PO Box 445, New York, NY 10159-0445
ZIMBABWE	International Socialist Organisation, PO Box 6758, Harare

The following issues of *International Socialism* (second series) are available price £3 (including postage) from IS Journal, PO Box 82, London E3 3LH. *International Socialism* 2:58 and 2:65 are available on cassette from the Royal National Institute for the Blind (Peterborough Library Unit). Phone 01733 370 777.

International Socialism 2:94 Spring 2002

Chris Harman: Argentina: rebellion at the sharp end of the world crisis ★ Martin Smith: The return of the rank and file? ★ Leo Zeilig: Crisis in Zimbabwe ★ Jim Wolfreys: Pierre Bourdieu: voice of resistance ★ Richard Greeman: Memoirs of a revolutionary ★ Dave Crouch: The seeds of national liberation ★

International Socialism 2:93 Special issue

John Rees: Imperialism: globalisation, the state and war ★ Jonathan Neale: The long torment of Afghanistan ★ Anne Alexander: The crisis in the Middle East ★ Mike Gonzalez: The poisoned embrace: Plan Colombia and the expansion of imperial power ★ Chris Harman: The new world recession ★

International Socialism 2:92 Autumn 2001

Tom Behan: 'Nothing can be the same again' ★ Boris Kagarlitsky: The road from Genoa ★ Alex Callinicos: Toni Negri in perspective ★ Jack Fuller: The new workerism: the politics of the Italian autonomists ★ Goretti Horgan: How does globalisation affect women? ★ Rumy Hasan: East Asia since the 1997 crisis ★ Charlie Kimber: Dark heart of imperialism ★ Megan Trudell: The pursuit of 'unbounded freedom' ★

International Socialism 2:91 Summer 2001

Susan George: What now? ★ Walden Bello: The global conjuncture ★ Chris Nineham: An idea whose time has come ★ Mike Marqusee: Labour's long march to the right ★ Mike Davis: Wild streets—*American Graffiti* versus the Cold War ★ Goretti Horgan: Changing women's lives in Ireland ★ John Lister: We will fight them in the hedgerows ★ Mike Gonzalez: The Zapatistas after the Great March—a postscript ★ Dragan Plavsic: Hoist on their own petards ★

International Socialism 2:90 Spring 2001

John Rees: Anti-capitalism, reformism and socialism ★ Chris Harman: Beyond the boom ★ Walden Bello: 2000: the year of global protest ★ Michael Lavalette and others: The woeful record of the House of Blair ★ Brian Manning: History and socialism ★ Peter Morgan: A troublemaker's charter ★

International Socialism 2:89 Winter 2000

Lindsey German: Serbia's spring in October ★ Anne Alexander: Powerless in Gaza: the Palestinian Authority and the myth of the 'peace process' ★ Boris Kagarlitsky: The lessons of Prague ★ Mike Gonzalez: The Zapatistas: the challenges of revolution in a new millennium ★ Stuart Hood: Memoirs of the Italian Resistance ★ Esme Choonara: Threads of resistance ★ Megan Trudell: Setting the record straight ★ Judy Cox: Reasons to be cheerful: theories of anti-capitalism ★ Mark O'Brien: A comment on *Tailism and the Dialectic* ★

International Socialism 2:88 Autumn 2000

Chris Harman: Anti-capitalism: theory and practice ★ Paul McGarr: Why green is red ★ Boris Kagarlitsky: The suicide of *New Left Review* ★ Gilbert Achcar: The 'historical pessimism' of Perry Anderson ★ Dave Renton: Class consciousness and the origins of Labour ★ Keith Flett: Socialists and the origins of Labour: some other perspectives ★ John Newsinger: Fantasy and revolution: an interview with China Miéville ★

International Socialism 2:87 Summer 2000

Lindsey German: How Labour lost its roots ★ Mark O'Brien: Socialists and the origins of Labour ★ Judy Cox: Skinning a live tiger paw by paw ★ Peter Morgan: The morning after the night before... ★ John Newsinger: Plumbing the depths: some recent books on New Labour ★ Abbie Bakan: From Seattle to Washington: the making of a movement ★ Jim Wolfreys: In perspective: Pierre Bourdieu ★ Nick Barrett: Complement to 'Reformism and class polarisation in Europe' ★ Mark Krantz: Humanitarian intentions on the road to hell ★ John Rees: Tony Cliff: theory and practice ★ Ygal Sarneh: A revolutionary life ★ Shaun Doherty: The language of liberation ★

International Socialism 2:86 Spring 2000
John Charlton: Talking Seattle ★ Abbie Bakan: After Seattle: the politics of the World Trade Organisation ★ Mark O'Brien: In perspective: Susan George ★ Rob Ferguson: Chechnya: the empire strikes back ★ Lindsey German: The Balkans' imperial problem ★ Megan Trudell: The Russian civil war: a Marxist analysis ★ Robin Blackburn: Reviewing the millennia ★ Jim Wolfreys: In defence of Marxism ★ Judy Cox: Can capitalism be sustained? ★

International Socialism 2:85 Winter 1999
Alex Callinicos: Reformism and class polarisation in Europe ★ Michael Lavalette and Gerry Mooney: New Labour, new moralism: the welfare politics and ideology of New Labour under Blair ★ Ken Coates: Benign imperialism versus United Nations ★ John Baxter: Is the UN an alternative to 'humanitarian imperialism'? ★ John Rose: Jesus: history's most famous missing person ★ Chris Harman: The 20th century: an age of extremes or an age of possibilities? ★ Mike Gonzalez: Is modernism dead? ★ Peter Morgan: The man behind the mask ★ Anne Alexander: All power to the imagination ★ Anna Chen: George Orwell: a literary Trotskyist? ★ Rob Hoveman: History of theory ★ Chris Harman: Comment on Molyneux on art ★

International Socialism 2:84 Autumn 1999
Neil Davidson: The trouble with 'ethnicity' ★ Jim Wolfreys: Class struggles in France ★ Phil Marfleet: Nationalism and internationalism ★ Tom Behan: The return of Italian Communism ★ Andy Durgan: Freedom fighters or Comintern army? The International Brigades in Spain ★ John Molyneux: Art, alienation and capitalism: a reply to Chris Nineham ★ Judy Cox: Dreams of equality: the levelling poor of the English Revolution ★

International Socialism 2:83 Summer 1999
John Rees: The socialist revolution and the democratic revolution ★ Mike Haynes: Theses on the Balkan War ★ Angus Calder: Into slavery: the rise of imperialism ★ Jim Wolfreys: The physiology of barbarism ★ John Newsinger: Scenes from the class war: Ken Loach and socialist cinema ★

International Socialism 2:82 Spring 1999
Lindsey German: The Blair project cracks ★ Dan Atkinson and Larry Elliott: Reflating Keynes: a different view of the crisis ★ Peter Morgan: The new Keynesians: staking a hold in the system? ★ Rob Hoveman: Brenner and crisis: a critique ★ Chris Nineham: Art and alienation: a reply to John Molyneux ★ Paul McGarr: Fascists brought to book ★ Brian Manning: Revisionism revised ★ Neil Davidson: In perspective: Tom Nairn ★

International Socialism 2:81 Winter 1998
Alex Callinicos: World capitalism at the abyss ★ Mike Haynes and Pete Glatter: The Russian catastrophe ★ Phil Marfleet: Globalisation and the Third World ★ Lindsey German: In a class of its own ★ Judy Cox: John Reed: reporting on the revolution ★ Kevin Ovenden: The resistible rise of Adolf Hitler ★

International Socialism 2:80 Autumn 1998
Clare Fermont: Indonesia: the inferno of revolution ★ Workers' representatives and socialists: Three interviews from Indonesia ★ Chris Bambery: Report from Indonesia ★ Tony Cliff: Revolution and counter-revolution: lessons for Indonesia ★ John Molyneux: The legitimacy of modern art ★ Gary McFarlane: A respectable trade? Slavery and the rise of capitalism ★ Paul McGarr: The French Revolution: Marxism versus capitalism ★ Shaun Doherty: Will the real James Connolly please stand up? ★

International Socialism 2:79 Summer 1998
John Rees: The return of Marx? ★ Lindsey German: Reflections on The Communist Manifesto ★ Judy Cox: An introduction to Marx's theory of alienation ★ Judith Orr: Making a comeback: the Marxist theory of crisis ★ Megan Trudell: New Labour, old conflicts: the story so far ★ John Molyneux: State of the art ★ Anna Chen: In perspective: Sergei Eisenstein ★ Jonathan Neale: Vietnam veterans ★ Phil Gasper: Bookwatch: Marxism and science ★

International Socialism 2:78 Spring 1998
Colin Sparks: The eye of the storm ★ Shin Gyoung-hee: The crisis and the workers' movement in South Korea ★ Rob Hoveman: Financial crises and the real economy ★ Peter Morgan: Class divisions in the gay community ★ Alex Callinicos: The secret of the dialectic ★ John Parrington: It's life, Jim, but not as we know it ★ Judy Cox: Robin Hood: earl, outlaw or rebel? ★ Ian Birchall: The vicelike hold of nationalism? A comment on Megan Trudell's 'Prelude to revolution' ★ William Keach: In perspective: Alexander Cockburn and Christopher Hitchens ★

International Socialism 2:77 Winter 1997
Audrey Farrell: Addicted to profit—capitalism and drugs ★ Mike Gonzalez: The resurrections of Che Guevara ★ Sam Ashman: India: imperialism, partition and resistance ★ Henry Maitles: Never again! ★ John Baxter: The return of political science ★ Dave Renton: Past its peak ★

International Socialism 2:76 Autumn 1997
Mike Haynes: Was there a parliamentary alternative in 1917? ★ Megan Trudell: Prelude to revolution: class consciousness and the First World War ★ Judy Cox: A light in the darkness ★ Pete Glatter: Victor Serge: writing for the future ★ Gill Hubbard: A guide to action ★ Chris Bambery: Review article: Labour's history of hope and despair ★

International Socialism 2:75 Summer 1997
John Rees: The class struggle under New Labour ★ Alex Callinicos: Europe: the mounting crisis ★ Lance Selfa: Mexico after the Zapatista uprising ★ William Keach: Rise like lions? Shelley and the revolutionary left ★ Judy Cox: What state are we really in? ★ John Parrington: In perspective: Valentin Voloshinov ★

International Socialism 2:73 Winter 1996
Chris Harman: Globalisation: a critique of a new orthodoxy ★ Chris Bambery: Marxism and sport ★ John Parrington: Computers and consciousness: a reply to Alex Callinicos ★ Joe Faith: Dennett, materialism and empiricism ★ Megan Trudell: Who made the American Revolution? ★ Mark O'Brien: The class conflicts which shaped British history ★ John Newsinger: From class war to Cold War ★ Alex Callinicos: The state in debate ★ Charlie Kimber: Review article: coming to terms with barbarism in Rwanda in Burundi ★

International Socialism 2:72 Autumn 1996
Alex Callinicos: Betrayal and discontent: Labour under Blair ★ Sue Cockerill and Colin Sparks: Japan in crisis ★ Richard Levins: When science fails us ★ Ian Birchall: The Babeuf bicentenary: conspiracy or revolutionary party? ★ Brian Manning: A voice for the poor ★ Paul O'Flinn: From the kingdom of necessity to the kingdom of freedom: Morris's *News from Nowhere* ★ Clare Fermont: Bookwatch: Palestine and the Middle East 'peace process' ★

International Socialism 2:71 Summer 1996
Chris Harman: The crisis of bourgeois economics ★ Hassan Mahamdallie: William Morris and revolutionary Marxism ★ Alex Callinicos: Darwin, materialism and revolution ★ Chris Nineham: Raymond Williams: revitalising the left? ★ Paul Foot: A passionate prophet of liberation ★ Gill Hubbard: Why has feminism failed women? ★ Lee Sustar: Bookwatch: fighting to unite black and white ★

International Socialism 2:70 Spring 1996
Alex Callinicos: South Africa after apartheid ★ Chris Harman: France's hot December ★ Brian Richardson: The making of a revolutionary ★ Gareth Jenkins: Why Lucky Jim turned right—an obituary of Kingsley Amis ★ Mark O'Brien: The bloody birth of capitalism ★ Lee Humber: Studies in revolution ★ Adrian Budd: A new life for Lenin ★ Martin Smith: Bookwatch: the General Strike ★

International Socialism 2:69 Winter 1995
Lindsey German: The Balkan war: can there be peace? ★ Duncan Blackie: The left and the Balkan war ★ Nicolai Gentchev: The myth of welfare dependency ★ Judy Cox: Wealth, poverty and class in Britain today ★ Peter Morgan: Trade unions and strikes ★ Julie Waterson: The party at its peak ★ Megan Trudell: Living to some purpose ★ Nick Howard: The rise and fall of socialism in one city ★ Andy Durgan: Bookwatch: Civil war and revolution in Spain ★

International Socialism 2:68 Autumn 1995
Ruth Brown: Racism and immigration in Britain ★ John Molyneux: Is Marxism deterministic? ★ Stuart Hood: News from nowhere? ★ Lee Sustar: Communism in the heart of the beast ★ Peter Linebaugh: To the teeth and forehead of our faults ★ George Paizis: Back to the future ★ Phil Marshall: The children of stalinism ★ Paul D'Amato: Bookwatch: 100 years of cinema ★

International Socialism 2:67 Summer 1995
Paul Foot: When will the Blair bubble burst? ★ Chris Harman: From Bernstein to Blair—100 years of revisionism ★ Chris Bambery: Was the Second World War a war for democracy? ★ Alex Callinicos: Hope against the Holocaust ★Chris Nineham: Is the media all powerful? ★ Peter Morgan: How the West was won ★ Charlie Hore: Bookwatch: China since Mao ★

International Socialism 2:66 Spring 1995
Dave Crouch: The crisis in Russia and the rise of the right ★ Phil Gasper: Cruel and unusual punishment: the politics of crime in the United States ★ Alex Callinicos: Backwards to liberalism ★ John Newsinger: Matewan: film and working class struggle ★ John Rees: The light and the dark ★ Judy Cox: How to make the Tories disappear ★ Charlie Hore: Jazz: a reply to the critics ★ Pat Riordan: Bookwatch: Ireland ★